finding heroes

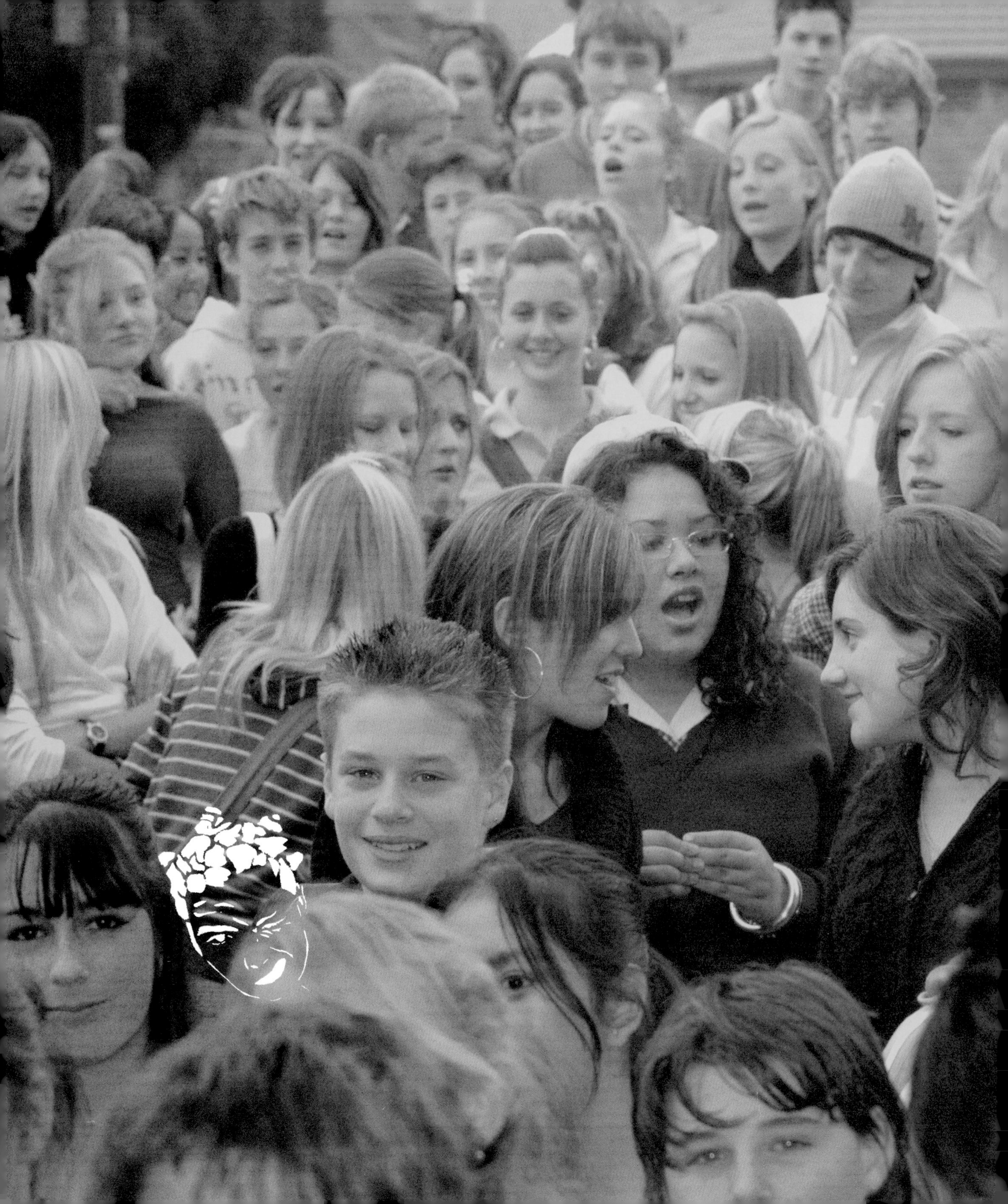

finding Heroes

Be inspired by stories of amazing journeys

Dr Jon Carnegie and Jim Stynes

ALLEN&UNWIN

First published in 2006

Allen & Unwin Pty Ltd
83 Alexander Street
Crows Nest NSW 2065
Australia

Phone: (61 2) 8425 0100
Fax: (61 2) 9906 2218
Email: info@allenandunwin.com
Web: www.allenandunwin.com

National Library of Australia
Cataloguing-in-publication entry:
Carnegie, Jon.

Finding heroes.

For children aged 8-12 years.
ISBN 1 74114 757 3.

1. Motivation (Psychology) - Juvenile literature. 2.
Children - Conduct of life - Juvenile literature. 3.
Achievement motivation in children - Case studies -
Juvenile literature. I. Stynes, Jim. II. Title.

155.4138

Designed and typeset by MAU Design
Front cover image of ballkids at the Australian Tennis Open 2006 courtesy of the Aviva Group and Fairfax
Edited by Eva Mills
Printed in Siingapore by Imago
10 9 8 7 6 5 4 3 2 1

contents

No dreamer is ever too small.
No dream is ever too big

CHAPTER ONE

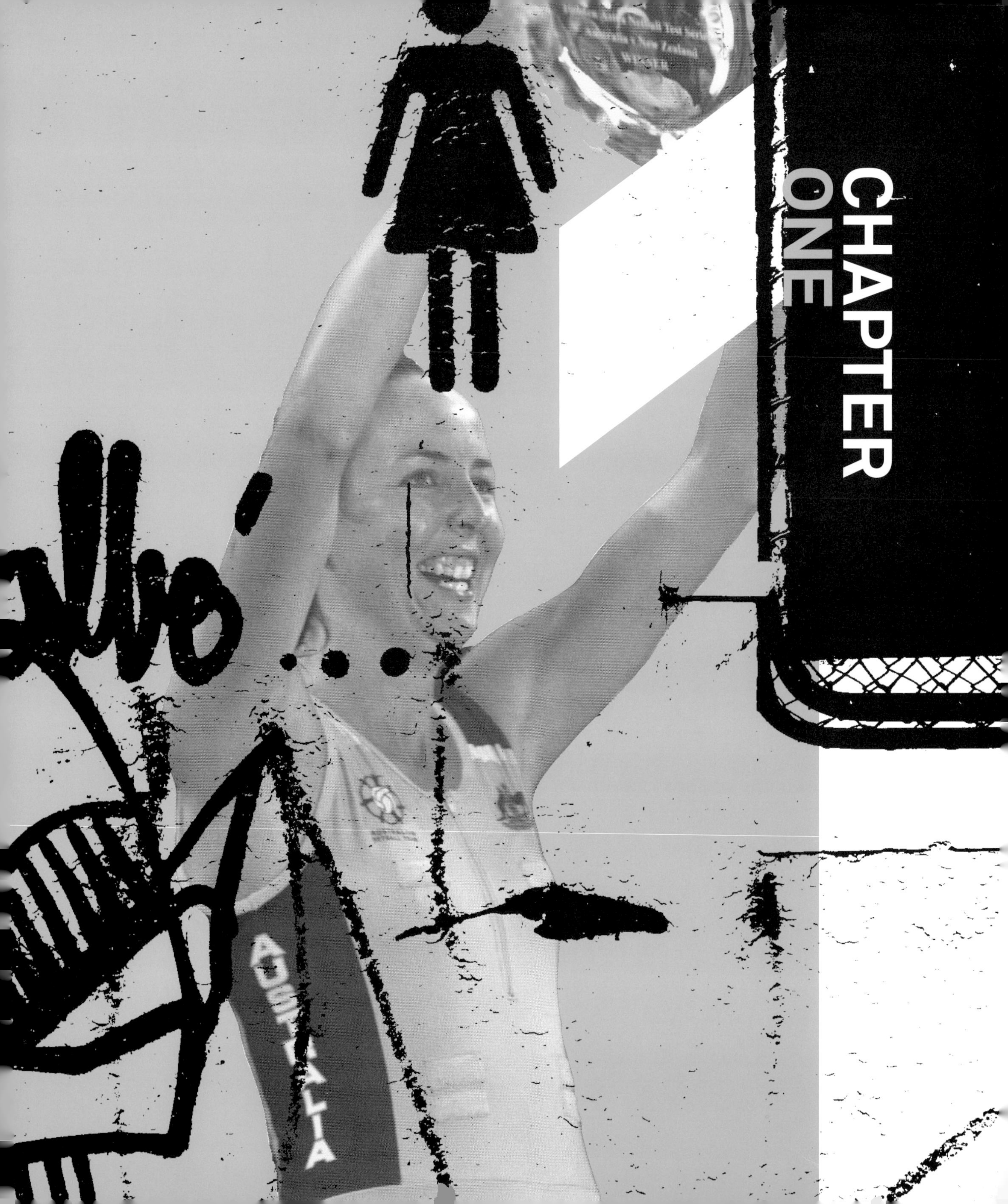
AUSTRALIA

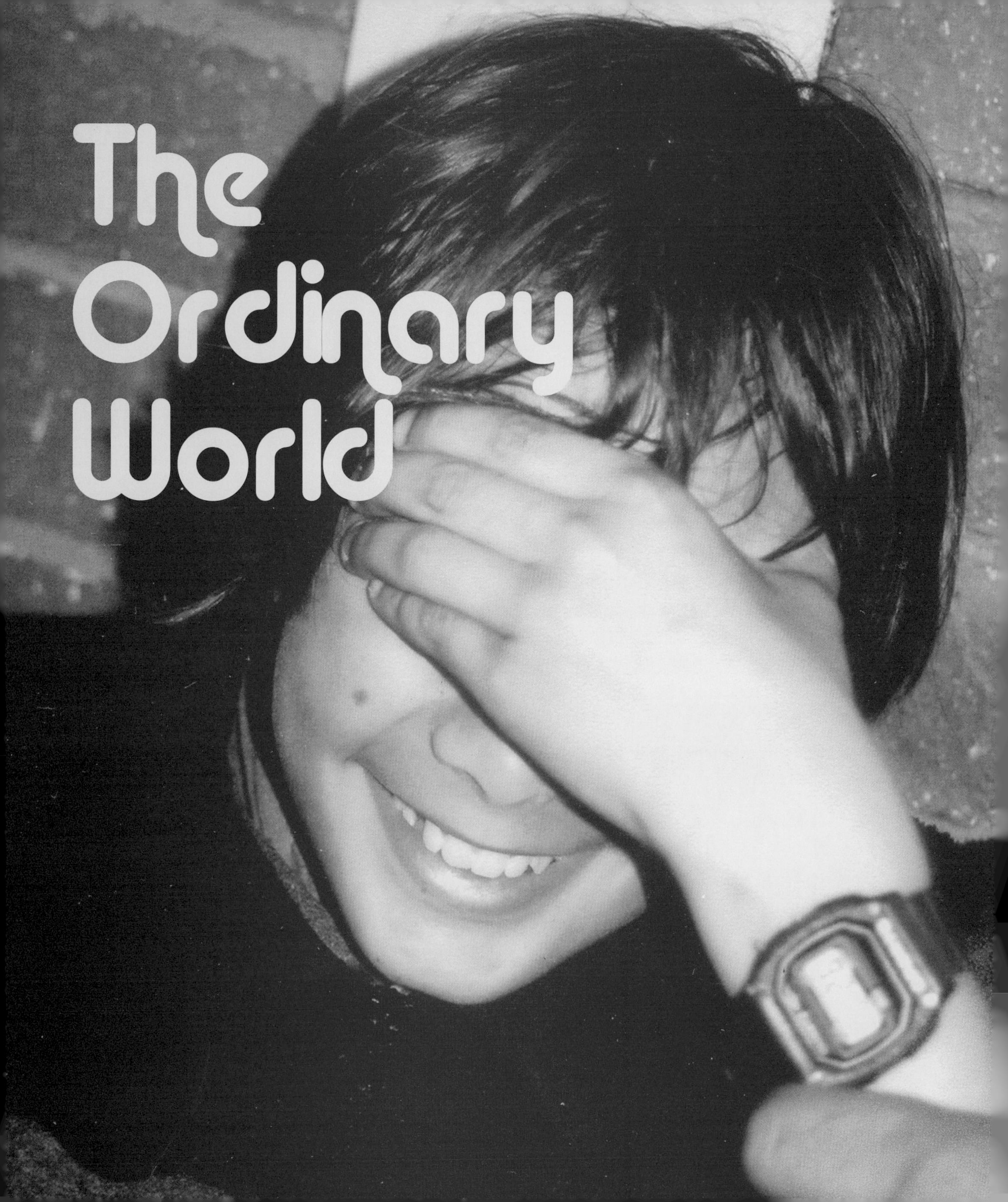
The Ordinary World

The ordinary world is a place where you can relax and feel safe. It is your everyday world, the place where you do the same things most days of your life.

It is also a place where you can dream of all the things you want to achieve in life. Perhaps your ordinary world is your bedroom at home. Perhaps it is a place you go on holidays. Or your ordinary world might even be a place in your mind.

If you've seen the movie Antz, you'll know what we mean. In Antz, the worker ants believe the world is just a place where you dig tunnels all day. But as they soon find out, the world is a lot more than that.

The ordinary world is a great place to be comfortable, but if we want to live big dreams, we all have to leave the ordinary world at some stage.

FILM:
ANTZ

Sometimes I think
I'm just not cut
out to be a worker...
The whole system
just... makes me
feel... insignificant.

Family

For most of us, our family is a big part of our ordinary world. Our mums and dads work hard to provide us with a safe place to live. Sometimes our parents don't live together and our ordinary world is in two houses. Some of us don't know our mums and dads and we live with other people. Whatever the case, for most people families are a great place to find safety and relaxation.

Friends

Friends are really important in the ordinary world. Good friends let you be yourself, they encourage you to be different, and they help you explore the world. Friends are important in the adventures of life as well. While your family gives you a safe starting place, it is your friends who will travel the journey with you. Notice how Frodo and Sam travel together in The Lord of the Rings, how Shrek goes everywhere with Donkey, and how Simba from The Lion King always has someone by his side.

Movies, Magazines and Television

Sometimes if we want to escape from the ordinary world, we go to the movies or watch television. If you watch carefully, most movies start in the ordinary world. Shrek lived in a swamp, Harry Potter lived with his aunt and uncle, Simba was born into a family of lions, even Nemo the clownfish never strayed far from home in the beginning. All these characters were safe in their ordinary worlds, but when adventure called out to them, they had to leave in order to live their dreams.

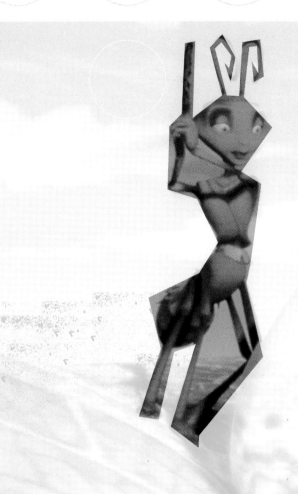

What is your ordinary world?

FILM: THE LION KING

Simba, I have given you all I can give. The journey is up to you now. I may not be there with you but I am inside you, with you all the way. Go now with the strength of your father.

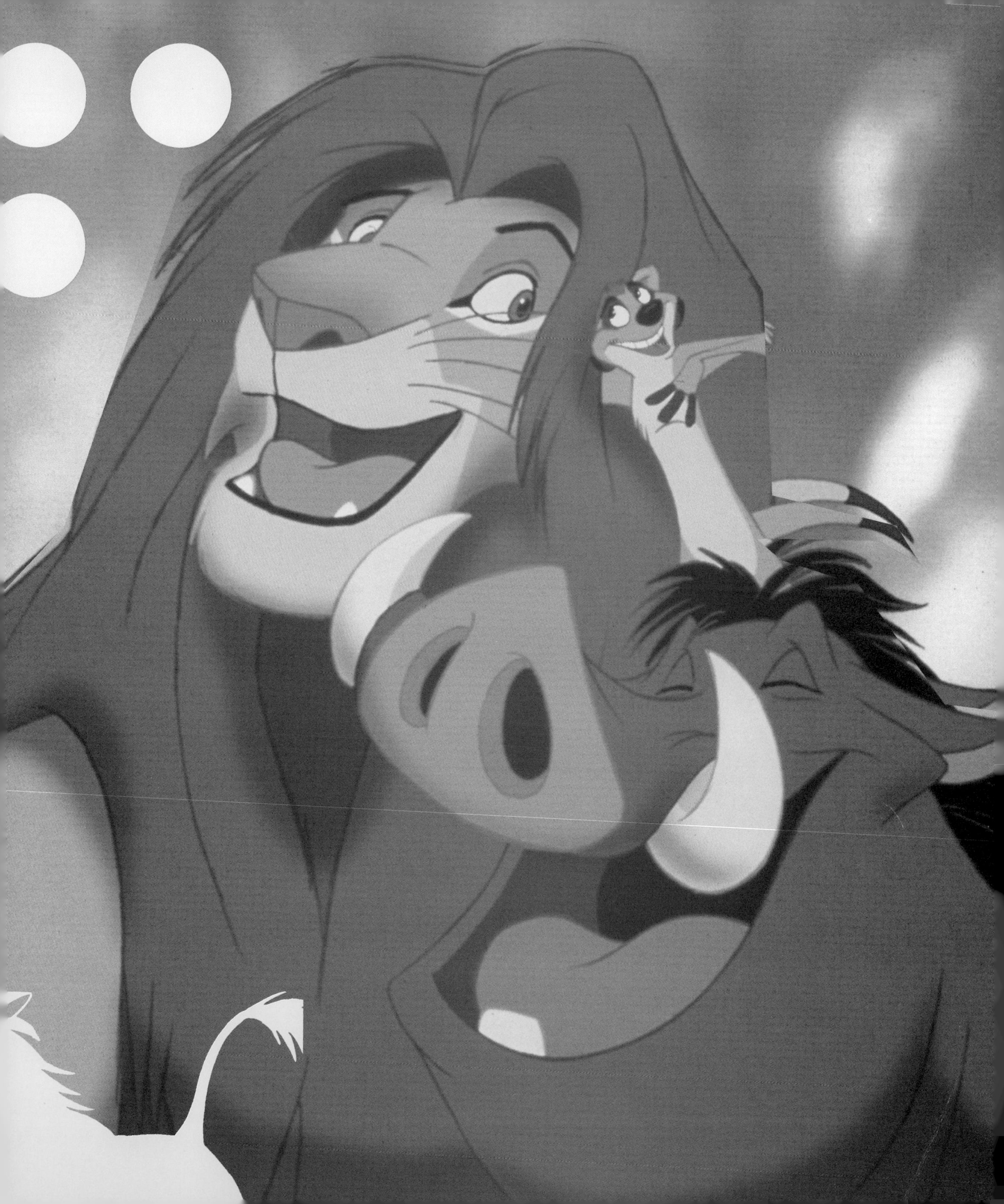

If it is so good, why leave the Ordinary World?

While the ordinary world might be comfortable, it's hard to have new experiences there, so after a while you stop learning about life if you stay.

Remember your first day at a new school? For some of us this was a really scary day, and we had fears which took us a while to overcome. Others coped okay with the first day — we felt we belonged right away, we made friends easily and enjoyed school right from the start.

But what would happen if we had to stay in Grade 1 all our lives? How would you feel if you had to keep repeating the same year over and over again with the same teacher? It seems stupid, right?

And yet, if you look closely, maybe that's exactly what your parents are doing! Some parents stay in the same job for 40 years. They live in the same house, and they go to the same place every holiday.

There are two reasons why this might happen. The first is that some parents are very happy in the ordinary world and don't need to get out. If you live in one of these families, you are lucky. The other reason is that a parent might become trapped in the ordinary world. Feeling trapped is really hard. Sometimes it seems impossible to move because of all the pressures from family, friends and the media to stay in the ordinary world.

When this happens it is time to start setting goals.

HERO:
LIZ ELLIS

Australian netballer Liz Ellis is a great goal setter. Not only does she score goals for the Australian netball team, she sets goals in her private life as well. Here she talks about some specific goals she kept in mind as Australia went into the last quarter of the deciding game of the World Netball Championship against New Zealand ...

From the first whistle both teams made it fairly clear that they would put everything on the line for the win. Bodies flew, pressure mounted ... We went into [the final] quarter six goals down – a deficit that we really had no right to make up in one 15 minute quarter.

I cannot remember precisely what was said in the team huddle before we went on, but our coach reminded us of all of the hard work we had put in [in] the lead up to this match. This match was the culmination of four years planning – four years of work dedicated to doing everything right in the last game of a tournament ... [watching] everything that goes in your mouth, not going to nightclubs and pubs too often because of the effect of the smoke, getting the right amount of sleep etc. for four years. I thought of all of the times my alarm had gone off at 6 am for me to get up and go and train before I went off to work. Of the sacrifices that I and my teammates had made in terms of our personal lives and our careers to get to this point.

Jill reminded us of our catchcry, 'whatever it takes'. She summed it up by saying 'no regrets'. No regrets ...

When I gave away a penalty close to the post 20 seconds before full time with the scores locked at 41 all, I thought that I would have a whole world full of regrets! As Donna Loffhagen took that shot, I promised myself that if that ball came out of the ring, no one on God's earth but me was going to get it. I kept that promise, the ball sped down court, Sharelle shot the most beautiful goal I have ever seen and then all hell broke loose. We had won.

Never have I felt such elation. How we did it, I don't know. I do know that persistence and determination [had] a lot to do with it ... We set ourselves a simple goal at the start of the final term – to get three turnovers. We focussed doggedly on the task at hand. As we began to come back I remember thinking that the Kiwis were beginning to look slightly panicked. I think they were too focussed on winning the World Championship rather than winning the game ...

To win with those girls was an enormous thrill ... We were absolutely overcome with the enormity of it all, and I laugh now at the photos of us rolling around on the court together.

Achieving your goals is one thing, achieving them with a group of people who have shared common experiences and made similar sacrifices only serves to increase that feeling of satisfaction when not only have you reached your goals, but you have achieved something beyond your wildest dreams ...

If you have a dream, do everything you can to fulfil it. Before the night of October 2, I had dreamed many times of holding up the 1999 World Championship trophy. During that game, particularly when we were seven goals down, those dreams began to look a little shaky, but I held on to them, and it was those dreams that kept me playing to the final whistle. It was what kept us going when things weren't going our way. I had visualised winning and the celebrations that would follow ... To actually do it was the greatest feeling ever.

GO AUSSIE GO!

Setting Goals

Can you imagine playing football or netball without any goalposts and nets at each end? What do you think would happen?

In life, we need goals to give us motivation — to give us a reason for action.

Have you ever really wanted to have something and had to wait for it? Perhaps a present for Christmas or a new bike for your birthday? Perhaps you have to do certain jobs around the house or get good marks at school before you are allowed to get your reward. Parents often set up a series of rewards until you reach your final goal.

How Do Goals Help?

By setting goals, you give your life direction. This means you have a reason for doing things, and in the end you get a reward.

An archer has a target so he has something to aim at. Imagine he had no target — the arrows could end up all over the place! This is the difference between going somewhere rather than just anywhere.

How Do You Set Goals?

The most important thing about setting goals is to write them down. Not writing your goals down is like having goals in a match but not keeping score. By writing your goals down, you can start to measure your success.

Start Small but Finish Big

Let's say your goal is to save $50 for a new game. At the start this goal might seem too big, but when you break it down into little pieces, it suddenly becomes easier. So instead of starting with the big goal of saving $50, try breaking it down into smaller goals like saving $5 per month for ten months.

How do you eat an elephant? One mouthful at a time!

Inch by inch it's a cinch, yard by yard it's hard.

MICHAEL'S STORY

I tried to save for a Razor scooter for 12 months. My parents were tight, and said I had to save up half. I spent the whole year trying to play with my friends who were given Razor scooters for Christmas, but it was hard because I had a bike and couldn't carry it when we went into shopping centres and stuff.

I hated the shopping centre because when we went in, they all had money to spend but because I was trying to save, I didn't have any.

That's when I started to steal stuff.

At first it was real easy. I stole CDs and then sold them to my friends for half price. I felt really popular and I was making money and having enough to spend as well.

It only took three weeks to get the money I needed for the scooter, but because I couldn't tell my parents where I got the money, I decided to try and get the lot, by stealing a whole lot of CDs.

Getting caught was the worst day of my life. I had six CDs stuffed up my jumper when the security guard grabbed me. He made me call my dad, who had to come down to the shopping centre and pick me up.

But the worst part was that I had to tell on my friends. All those guys who bought CDs from me got in trouble too. Now I still don't have a scooter, and none of my friends talk to me either.

HERO:
ANNE FRANK

Anne Frank was born in Frankfurt am Main, Germany, on 12 June 1929. She had a sister, Margot, who was three years older than her. In 1933 Anne, Margot, her father (Otto Frank) and her mother (Edith Frank) moved to Amsterdam.

On Anne Frank's thirteenth birthday she received a diary which she liked best of all the presents she received that day. She named the diary 'Kitty' and loved to write in it. Anne's family was Jewish, and at this time in Amsterdam the Nazis were taking over the city and enforcing anti-Jewish rules. Anne hated these rules. She went to a Montessori school, but because of the anti-Jewish laws, she was moved to a Jewish lyceum where she quickly started to adjust.

When World War II started, Anne's father, Otto Frank, created a hiding place in an annex to his office with the help of some of the clients where he worked. The family moved into the hiding place as soon as possible.

One day in August 1944, a little after two years of hiding, the Frank family was found and put into a concentration camp. Anne died in Bergen-Belsen concentration camp of typhus at the age of fifteen. Anne's sister Margot also died of typhus. Her mother died of starvation, and her father was the only one of the Frank family who survived.

While Anne was in hiding, she kept writing in her diary because she wanted to be educated. Her father Otto managed to keep her diary safe and, two years after she died, in 1947, her father published it unchanged. Anne Frank is remembered in many ways: books have been written about her, and plays and movies tell her story. In her short life she was able to write short stories and some short fables. But Anne Frank is most remembered for her diary, which has been published in over 30 languages.

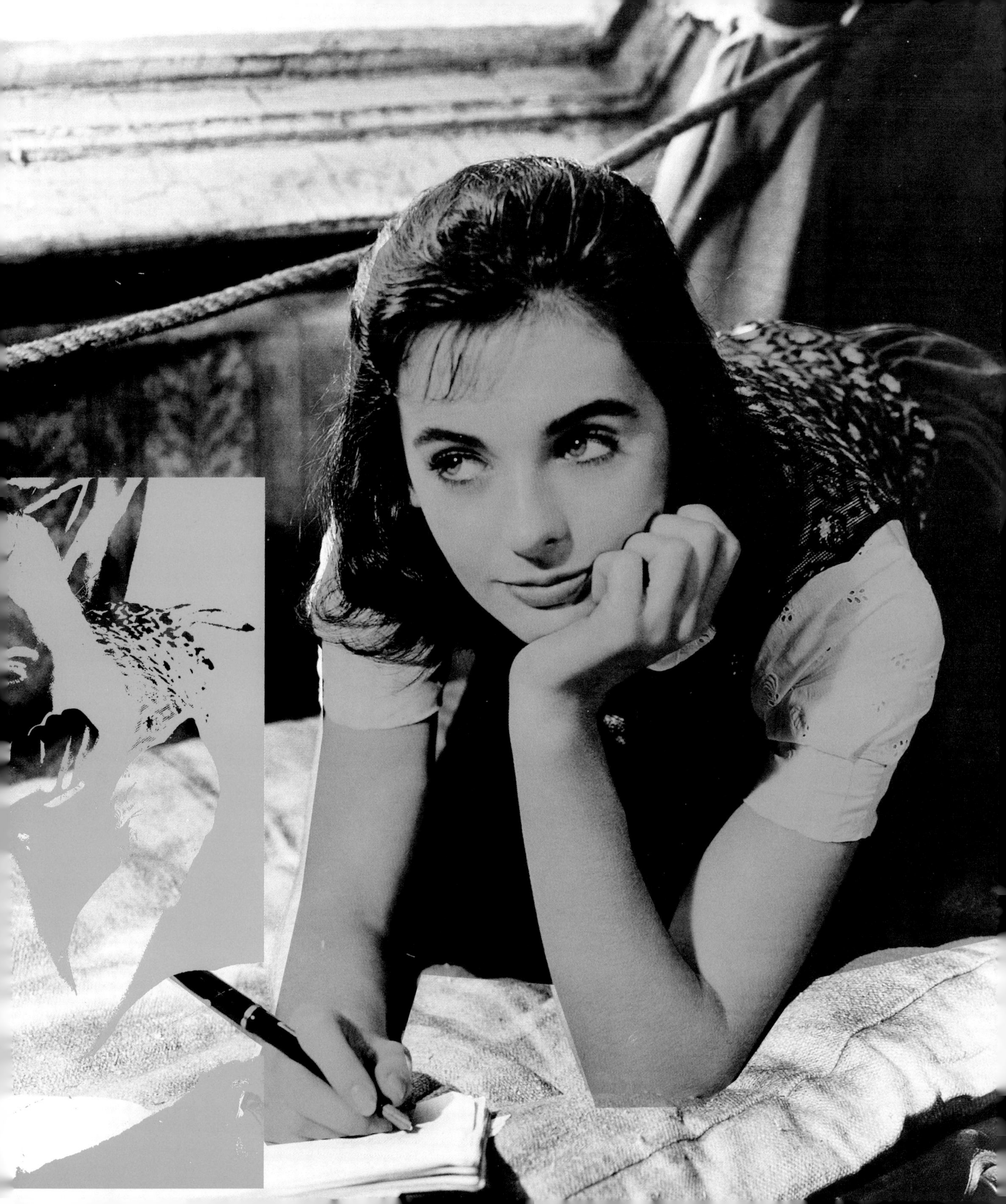

Find a Purpose

The final phase of leaving the ordinary world is to discover a reason why you should leave. Sometimes this is very hard, because you are having great fun in the ordinary world. If this is the case, don't be in too much of a hurry. If you are having fun and you are happy where you are, then you don't need to look elsewhere.

But if you feel there is more to life than you are getting at the moment, it might be time to try something new.

The first step to finding a purpose is to discover who you are. Some people spend their whole lives trying to figure this out. Try starting by making a list of the things you really love doing, and then try to explain why you love doing them.

There are three things you should note about a purpose:

- There is a purpose on the outside
- There is also a purpose on the inside
- There is a reward for achieving your purpose.

An outside purpose might be to get five As in your next school report. No question, this is a good purpose which will require lots of effort. If you reach your goal, you will see five As written on your report. But now imagine for a minute that you could not show that report to anyone ... so even your teacher wouldn't know you got five As!

How would that make you feel?

This leads us to our second purpose which is most often the real one. It's not the five As which make you feel good, it's the way those around you react when you get the five As. Your mum is pleased, your dad is proud and your big sister is jealous! But inside you feel good because you know how hard it was to get the results you were after.

Amazingly, the good feeling inside is often enough of a reward. Sometimes you get given a treat or a present when you do well and achieve a goal, but if the goal is truly worth achieving, the real gift is the way it makes you feel when you achieve it.

Is it time to try something new?

What Happens when I Fail?

Failure is just a part of learning. Anyone who does really well all the time is not aiming for hard enough dreams, and it is impossible to live big dreams without failing. So the question is not, 'What happens if I fail?'. The question is, 'What happens if I don't?'!

No matter how big or small you are, it's time to start setting goals and achieving dreams. Remember Charlie and the Chocolate Factory? Charlie's ordinary world is difficult. His family is poor, and it would be easy for Charlie to stop dreaming, but he doesn't.

He wants to leave his ordinary world and have an adventure. The chance to find a golden ticket in a chocolate bar is his opportunity, and he never stops believing he might find one. He even uses all his paper round money in pursuit of his goal.

Most of us wish, but don't take action.

Dreams don't come easy

Just setting goals is not enough, you also have to work hard at making them come true.

SUMMARY: THE ORDINARY WORLD

- The ordinary world is the comfort zone of life
- Family and friends support you in the ordinary world
- To continue learning, sometimes we must leave the ordinary world
- Setting goals gives us a reason for action
- Dreams don't come easy
- It takes courage to be who you are
- Failure is also part of learning
- Find a purpose

CHAPTER TWO

*The call
to adventure*

Resilience= inner strength

It can help you meet challenges even when you are scared or uncertain

The Call to Adventure

Sometimes in life we are asked to do things which we find a real challenge. Like the first day at a new school, or playing in a big sports match.

No matter how scared or nervous we might be, these moments are a chance to learn. In *The Lord of the Rings*, Frodo is unsure if he can carry the responsibility of 'the ring' and yet, as the journey continues, he learns that he has talents he never knew were inside him.

The same thing is true for you. Challenges in life call out to test us. Sometimes we get into trouble over something which wasn't our fault, sometimes we lose something valuable and have to own up to it, sometimes we are asked to do something new and we doubt if we can.

When you get calls like this there is no point being scared. Instead we must learn to develop **resilience**. Resilience is inner strength, and it can help you meet challenges even when you are scared or uncertain.

Resilience allows you to find friends who can help, it helps you to get through the tough times, and most of all it helps you to bounce back when you fail ... and fail you will.

Let's look at the story of Frodo again. As a hobbit, it was not in Frodo's nature to go on great adventures, yet he alone in the Council of Elrond stands up amid all the fuss and says, 'I will take it, I will take the ring though I do not know the way.'

Choosing to try new things often takes a brave step at the start. To join a ballet class or gymnastics club, to ride a horse or swim in the surf, to choose a new subject at school or go on a camp with people you don't know: all these things take courage.

Often when we hear a call to adventure we make excuses for not listening to it. When auditions for the school play are on, we might pretend we have too much homework to do. When the swimming sports come around, we might pretend to have an injury so we can't compete. When a big test is on a certain day, we might pretend to be sick so we don't have to go to school.

All these things are normal responses and everyone does them once in a while. But when they become habits, they can really restrict our lives.

As Gandalf says to Frodo, 'You really are an amazing creature.' And you are. The secret is having the courage to find out just how amazing.

I love the pain tolerance. I love the mental challenge of having to push yourself to the absolute extremes.

GRANT HACKETT

To find out how amazing we are, we have to keep trying new things when we get the chance. But this does not mean we will always be successful. In fact, as Olympic swimmer Grant Hackett says, it often takes a huge amount of hard work before our efforts are rewarded.

This is why it is really important for us to learn how to cope with hard or stressful times.

SARAH'S STORY

Sarah tells the story of the first time she had to sing in a school play.

'I was so nervous before our first dress rehearsal. Up until then we had only really spoken the song, but now we had to sing it. All my friends seemed so confident, but I just knew my voice would stand out. So when the time came, I thought I would sing the words as softly as I could, and let the others do the singing for me.

The worst part was, the other girls did the same thing. Everyone was too scared to sing loudly and so no one did. Our teacher made us do it twice. And then she made us do it a third time, and it was pretty loud by then and it sounded good.

I'll never forget after that she said, 'Why didn't you just sing like that in the first place?'

life is a challenge

HERO:
MARTIN LUTHER KING

One of the most famous calls to adventure in modern history came from US civil rights campaigner Martin Luther King in his 'I have a dream' address in 1964.

Despite the unfair circumstances under which Martin Luther King lived, he still managed to find the resilience and strength to stand up to forces that were bigger than he was. When he did this, many other people gained the confidence to stand up as well.

This can happen in your schoolyard too. Just like Martin Luther King had a dream that blacks and whites could live together in peace, so too do we have a dream that schools can exist without bullying. Sometimes your call to adventure is to support a friend who is being picked on. And as Martin Luther King proved, when one person is prepared to stand up against a bully, other people might gain the confidence to stand up as well. Your call to adventure can lead to changing the way other people act.

I have a dream.

It is a dream deeply rooted in the American dream.

I have a dream that one day our nation will rise up and live out the true meaning of its creed: 'We hold these truths to be self evident that all men are created equal.'

I have a dream that on the red hills of Georgia, the sons of former slaves and the sons of former slave owners will be able to sit at the table of brotherhood.

I have a dream that one day, even in the state of Mississippi, a state sweltering from the heat of injustice, sweltering from the heat of oppression, will be transformed into an oasis of freedom and justice.

I have a dream that my four little children will one day live in a nation where they will not be judged by the colour of their skin but by the content of their character.

I have a dream today …

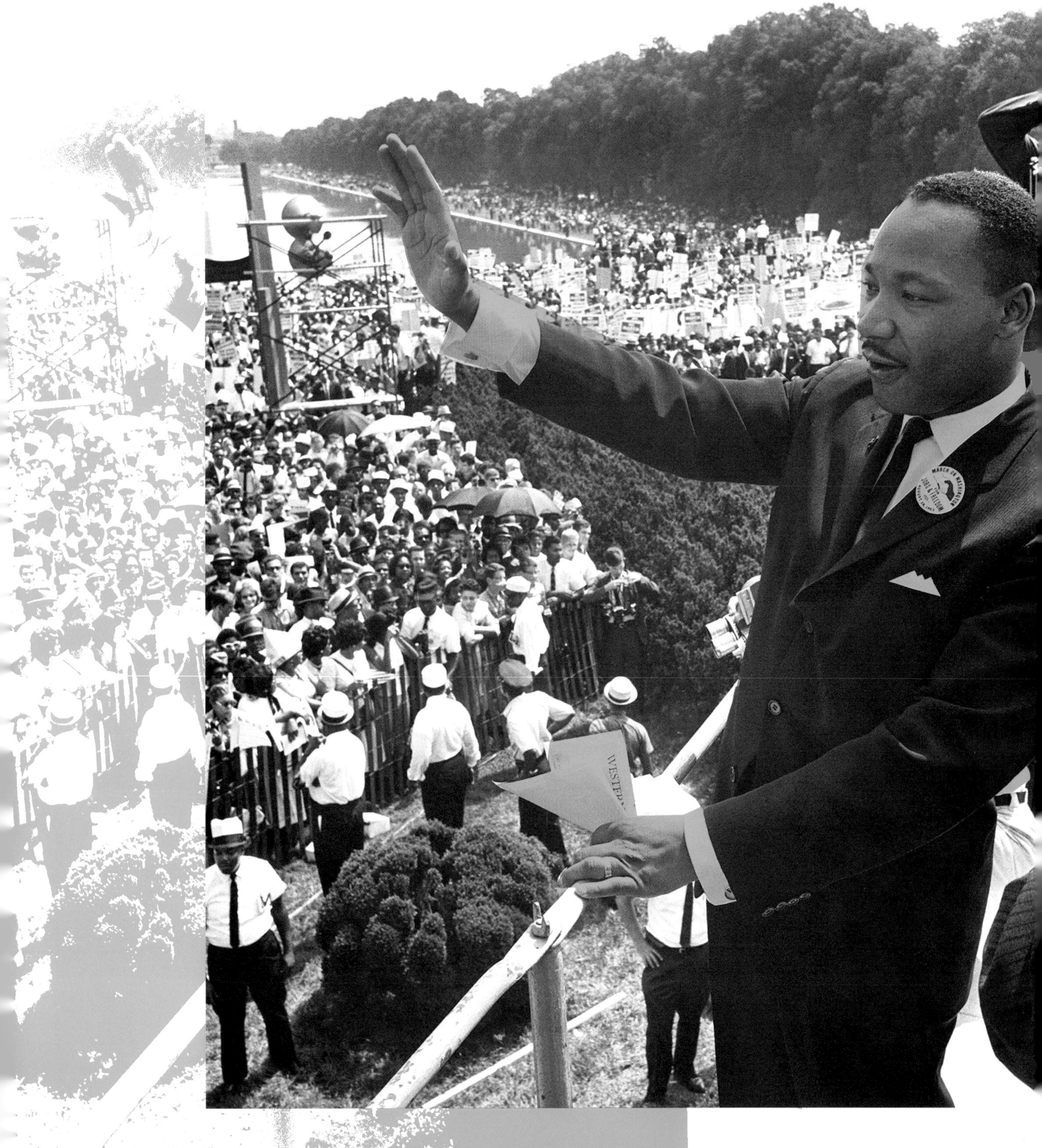

Listen for the Right Call

Of course, just because someone asks you to do something doesn't mean you have to follow them.

Strangers and people you do not trust might ask you to follow them, and the results can be awful. If you have any doubt about what you have been asked to do by anyone, you should always seek advice and help from someone you trust before making the decision.

Unfortunately there are people in the world who may say they want to help you or give you something, but in the end they are only interested in taking things away from you. We live in a world were young people have to be careful. The best way to recognise the right call is to learn to trust our instinct. As soon as we feel something is wrong, we need to find the courage to walk away.

ASHLEY'S STORY

'My friend Anna has an older sister who is always trying to get me and Anna to do stuff with her. At first it started out as a bit of fun. We used to go to the shopping centre with her and do dares. But the dares got worse and worse until one day she dared me to steal a video game from the video store.

She called me chicken if I didn't do it, and she even said she would tell my mum all the other bad stuff I did.

I didn't know what to do, so I stole the video game. It was easy in the end, but I felt bad about it all day, so I told my mum what had happened. I didn't know how she would react, but I couldn't believe how cool she was. She was mad I had stolen, but after I returned the video game, she said she had never been more proud of me in my life.'

How Do You Know when to Follow the Call?

The more experience we get in life, the more we learn to trust our instincts. Instincts are built-in feelings that help you judge what is right and what is wrong.

For example, imagine yourself walking down the street and seeing a blind person drop $50 on the ground. What would you do? For most of us, our instinct would be to pick it up and give it back to the blind person.

It's a bit like when you are running along at full speed and suddenly an object is thrust in front of you. Your instinct is to raise your hands to protect your face and head. This happens for a reason: the face and head are the most easily hurt areas of the body.

The same thing happens in life. Your instinct, or conscience as some people call it, is designed to help you decide what is right and wrong.

Sometimes the decision is clear-cut, like giving the $50 back to the blind person, but other times it is very hard to make. For example, what if you found the $50 in the schoolyard? What would you do then? Some of us may call out, asking if anyone had dropped it, others may take it to the principal's office or give it to a teacher and ask if anyone had been looking for it. Many would keep it.

What would you do? And how would you 'know' if it was the right thing to do?

Refusing the Call

Throughout the journey of life, you will be faced with difficult calls to adventure. Each of these calls requires you to act differently. Some require you to take a risk, others require you to overcome great fear, but in the end they all require you to **act**.

The best way to act is get advice and help from people you trust, but unfortunately what most of us do is create excuses instead.

At the time the excuse might not seem like an excuse at all.

DAVID'S STORY

David tells the story of how he was picked on by his older brother all the time.

'Whenever no one was looking he used to hit me, until it made a bruise on my arm and my leg. It really hurt, but he just used to say I was weak, and that if I told Mum or Dad he would do it even more.

At the time that seemed like a pretty good reason not to tell Mum and Dad, but now that I look back I realise it was an excuse. I didn't want to tell Dad because I thought he would think I was weak as well. So I kept letting it happen.

I used to daydream about standing up to my brother and hitting him back, but I never did. Instead I just let it go on and on. It wasn't until my dad saw me in the swimming pool one day that he asked how I got the bruises. My brother was there and he stared at me like he would kill me if I said anything. So I told a lie. I said I got them playing cricket.

When Dad was gone my brother came up to me and punched me, saying I was lucky I didn't tell. But I didn't feel that lucky at all. He is still punching me today.

If you were in David's situation, what would you do?'

In *The Lord of the Rings* when Gandalf says to Frodo that he never ceases to be amazed by hobbits, what he is really saying is that hobbits have unknown sources of power.

This is the same for us as well. We are a bit like an iceberg, where only a little bit pokes out of the water and the rest is underneath. The bit that most people see is just the tip - what lies beneath is the base.

When a call to adventure arrives, we need to test the call on a number of levels first:

- Is it safe?
- Do I trust the person making the call?
- Does it feel right?
- Who can help me?
- Am I making excuses for not acting?
- How can this adventure help unlock the hidden me which lies beneath the surface?

FILM:
THE LORD OF THE RINGS

The Ordinary World

Frodo's ordinary world is the safe village in which he was born and raised. As a hobbit, Frodo does not stray far from safety and is destined to live a life of peace and harmony, just as his ancestors had done.

The Call to Adventure

However, one day Frodo is given a mysterious ring, by the only hobbit he knows who has ever been on an adventure. The ring has mysterious powers, and if it were ever to fall into the hands of the Dark Lord Sauron, the world would be plunged into war and darkness. The only way to stop the power of the ring is to throw it into the fires of Mordor. So Frodo and his friends must leave their safe little village to go on an adventure.

The Special World

Frodo's special world is the treacherous landscape of Middle Earth, across which he and his companions must pass if they are to find the fires of Mordor.

Allies and Enemies

Along the way, Frodo is befriended by two humans named Aragorn and Boromir, an elf named Legolas and a dwarf named Gimli. Together with his hobbit friends and the ancient wizard Gandalf, the group are forced to face the evil powers of the orcs and the ringwraiths. The group must also face the enemy within each of them, which is the very force of darkness itself.

Tests and Challenges

As if all this was not testing enough, Frodo and his group must also face the evil wizard Saruman who is determined to kill them and gain power with the ring. Frodo and his companions are themselves often tested by the ring itself, which if worn brings ultimate power to the wearer.

Slaying the Dragon

Frodo has to 'slay the dragon' in many ways during the journey. First he must overcome his hobbit-like nature which encourages him not to be adventurous. Finally he has to overcome his fear of the ring itself.

The Reward

In the end Frodo and his friends gain the reward of knowing that friendship and courage have managed to overcome the forces of darkness and evil.

SUMMARY: THE CALL TO ADVENTURE

- *The call to adventure will come to you in many disguises, many times over*
- *Life is a challenge, and many people who have accomplished great things in their lives have done so not in spite of serious setbacks, but because of them*
- *Live life without regrets and value those close to you*
- *Follow your instincts and listen for the call*
- *Your real power lies in who you are*
- *Everyone is born with a gift; your journey is to discover it*

But we're chickens... we can't fly.

CHAPTER THREE

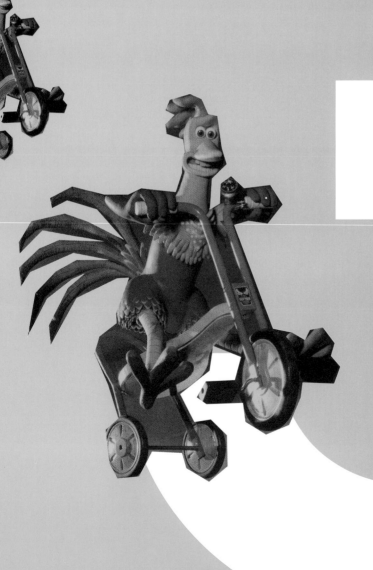

THE SPECIAL WORLD

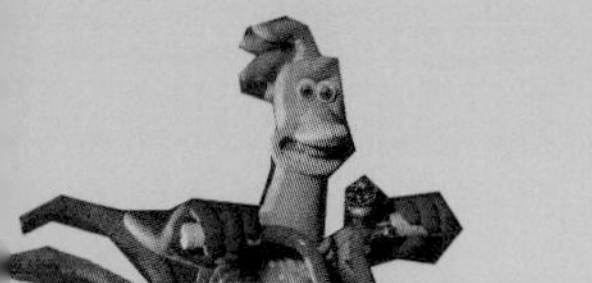
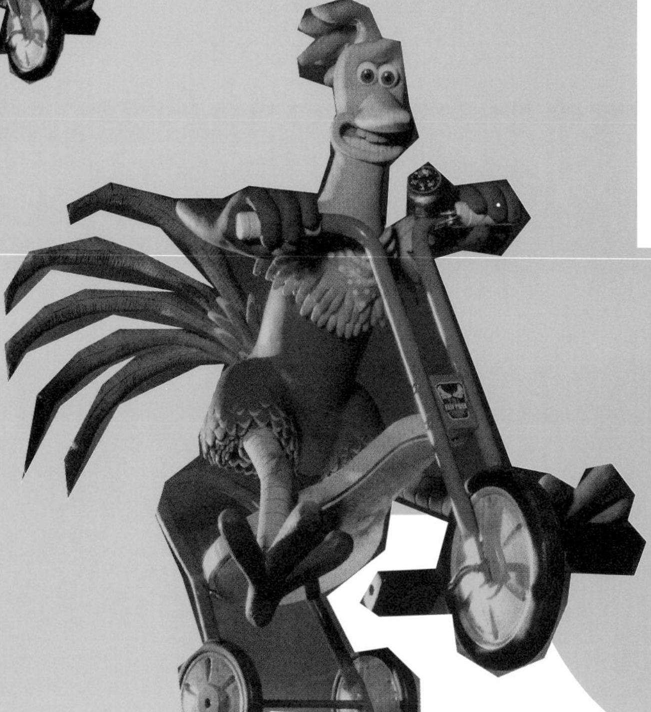
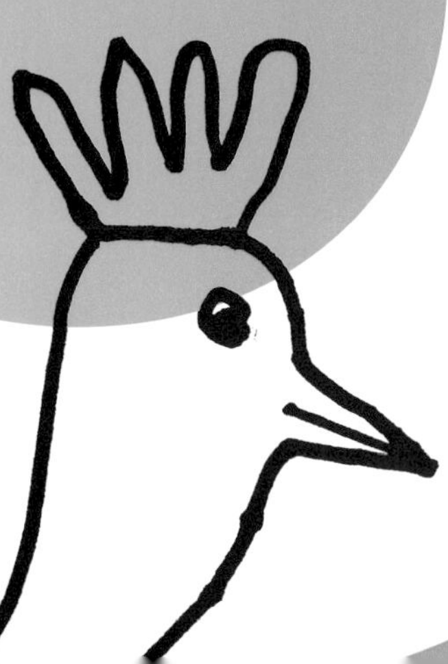

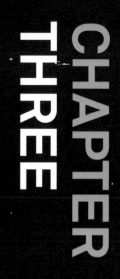

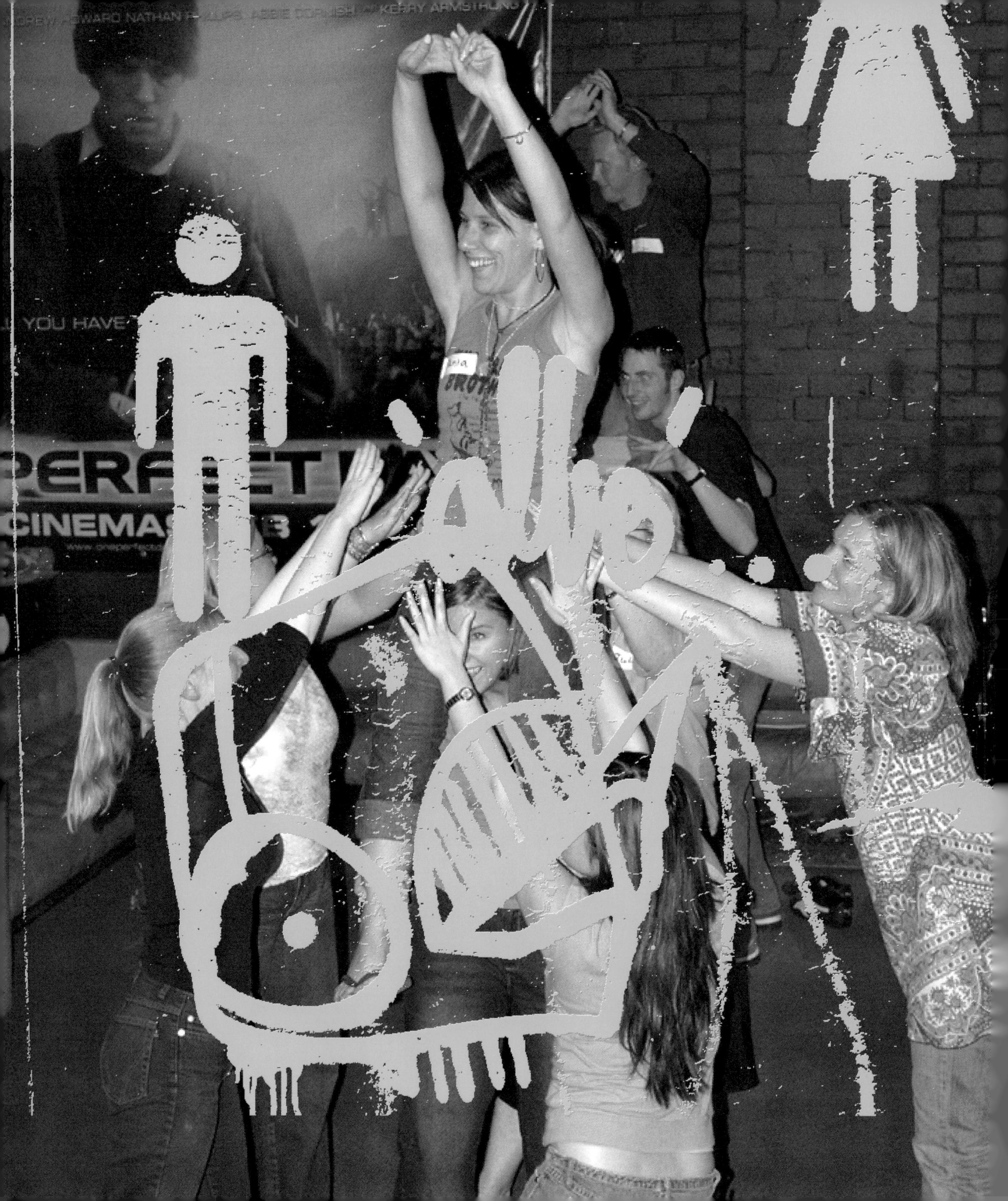

CINEMAS

The Special World

The special world is any place we enter for the first time. Often we are filled with excitement and sometimes we are filled with fear. But doing new things is all a part of the journey, and as we get older, doing these things alone becomes part of the journey as well.

The special world is not always a good place. Sometimes we are put into situations we don't like and we have to put up with them. For example, if we fall over and break a leg, we will find ourselves in the special world of hospital which may not be much fun at all. Or perhaps our family will win a trip to Disneyland, in which case our special world might be fantastic.

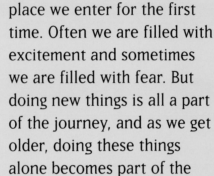

The thing to remember about the special world is that it often chooses us. We don't always have control over where we end up, but we do always have control over how we respond.

Every Journey Begins with a Single Step

In the movie *The Wizard of Oz*, Dorothy has to make a choice: whether to stay in Munchkinland where she is a hero or take a new adventure to the land of Oz alone. Going to Oz is scary. It would be easier for her to stay in Munchkinland and just complain about not being able to go home to Kansas, which is what many people would do.

This is the same with life. We will always find ourselves in situations we don't like, and when we do we have two choices: we can either complain about it and blame others, or we can take the first step to go out and find a better place.

Taking the first step can be hard, but without it we will never get anywhere.

JARROD'S STORY

Jarrod tells the story of when he first learned to ride a dirt bike.

> 'I loved dirt bikes and I really wanted to have a go on one but when I saw one up close on my friend's farm it just seemed really dangerous. Even though my friend's dad was showing me how to ride it, I could hardly hear what he was saying. All I could think about was the bike getting out of control and me falling off and being hurt really badly. What made it worse is that three of my friends were there and they all knew how to ride the bikes because they'd been to the farm a few times before.
>
> Once I was on the bike and felt the throttle in my hand I started to feel great. My friend's dad was helping me, and then he let me go and I actually felt like I had control. '

Confidence comes from experience. If Jarrod had never made the decision to get on the dirt bike, he would never have discovered how much he likes riding it around the farm. Since that day, Jarrod has had some scary moments. He still can't master everything about the bike but he keeps trying, and that's all we can ask of ourselves.

So, once you've established what your special world is ... take the first step!

The Special World Is Both a Positive and Negative Place

One of the hardest things about taking the first step is that we don't know where this journey will lead us. Remember the first time you ever got onto a really scary ride, or jumped off a high diving board? What did you learn? Usually we either hate the experience or we love it! That first step was so hard. If we hated the experience, at least now we know not to do things like that again. If we loved the experience, chances are we will want to do it again, only this time higher or faster!

One of the most important things to learn on our journey through life is that there are no failures ... there are only experiences. So as long as we learn from them, these experiences become the most valuable things in the world.

Accept or Reject the Journey

Sometimes the special world is not a place you should be. For example, every year in Australia young people drown because they do not swim between the flags at the beach. Some people see it as 'cool' to swim in dangerous places, but **there is a big difference between 'cool' and dangerous.**

Learning to make good decisions about where you go and who you go with is a big part of growing up. There are always people and circumstances out in the world that could hurt you. This is a fact of life. It is not something we should be afraid of, but something we must learn to recognise and deal with.

Taking risks is part of life, so learning which risks are worth taking is essential if we are going to live a good life.

How Do You Know If It's a Good Risk ?

To learn which special worlds are worth exploring and which ones are better left alone, the following steps can help:

- Ask someone you trust to go with you.
- Tell someone you trust where you are going.
- Talk about your adventure with someone who has been there before you.
- Ask your parents about it.
- Read books about it.
- Try breaking big journeys into little steps.
- Try riding a pony before you ride a horse.
- Try batting with a tennis ball before you use a cricket ball.
- Try jumping off the low board before you try the high board.

Accepting Responsibility

As a young person, we often spend our time blaming others for the trouble we get into. This is definitely a habit worth dropping.

Whingeing and crying when things go wrong does not help. Blaming others helps even less. The best way to cope is to say to yourself, 'Right, it might not be my fault I am in this mess, but I am certainly going to take responsibility for getting myself out of it.'

In life, unfair things happen all the time, and the best thing we can do is accept responsibility and work hard to change the situation we find ourselves in.

Not everything that happens to you is your fault; but it becomes your responsibility to act, to do something about it.

FIVE STATEMENTS TO AVOID IN LIFE

Justification

When you get upset about something, saying 'who cares, it's only a stupid game' is not an option.

Denial

When you get blamed for something you played a part in, saying 'it wasn't me' is not an option.

Laying Blame

When you and a friend get caught doing something wrong, saying 'it was all his fault' is not an option. Own up! Or when you fail a class test, saying 'it was all the teacher's fault' is not an option.

Quitting

When you have tried something and it hasn't worked the first time, saying 'I give up' is not an option.

'Life is not fair'

No matter what people will try to tell you, life is NOT fair. Sometimes we get blamed for stuff that wasn't our fault. Sometimes bad luck means we don't get the rewards we deserve. The quicker we accept this, the easier it is to get on with all the good stuff.

RESPONSIBILITY = ABILITY TO RESPOND

HERO: LOUISE SAUVAGE

Consider the story of wheelchair athlete Louise Sauvage. Born with a spinal condition known as myelodysplasia, Louise spent much of her teenage life in hospitals, having metal rods surgically inserted into her spine. It took her over two years to recover, after which she took up swimming and track and road racing.

It would have been easy for Louise to drop her bundle and give up on life, to claim to be one of the victims. Instead she turned her misfortune into success. As an athlete, she never laid blame on others or tried to justify quitting because of her spinal condition.

Her achievements are almost too many to list, but include world championships, Olympic gold medals and world records. Suffice to say that if Louise Sauvage had won gold medals in the same events at the Barcelona and Sydney Olympics as she did at the Paralympics, she would certainly be regarded as our greatest ever athlete!

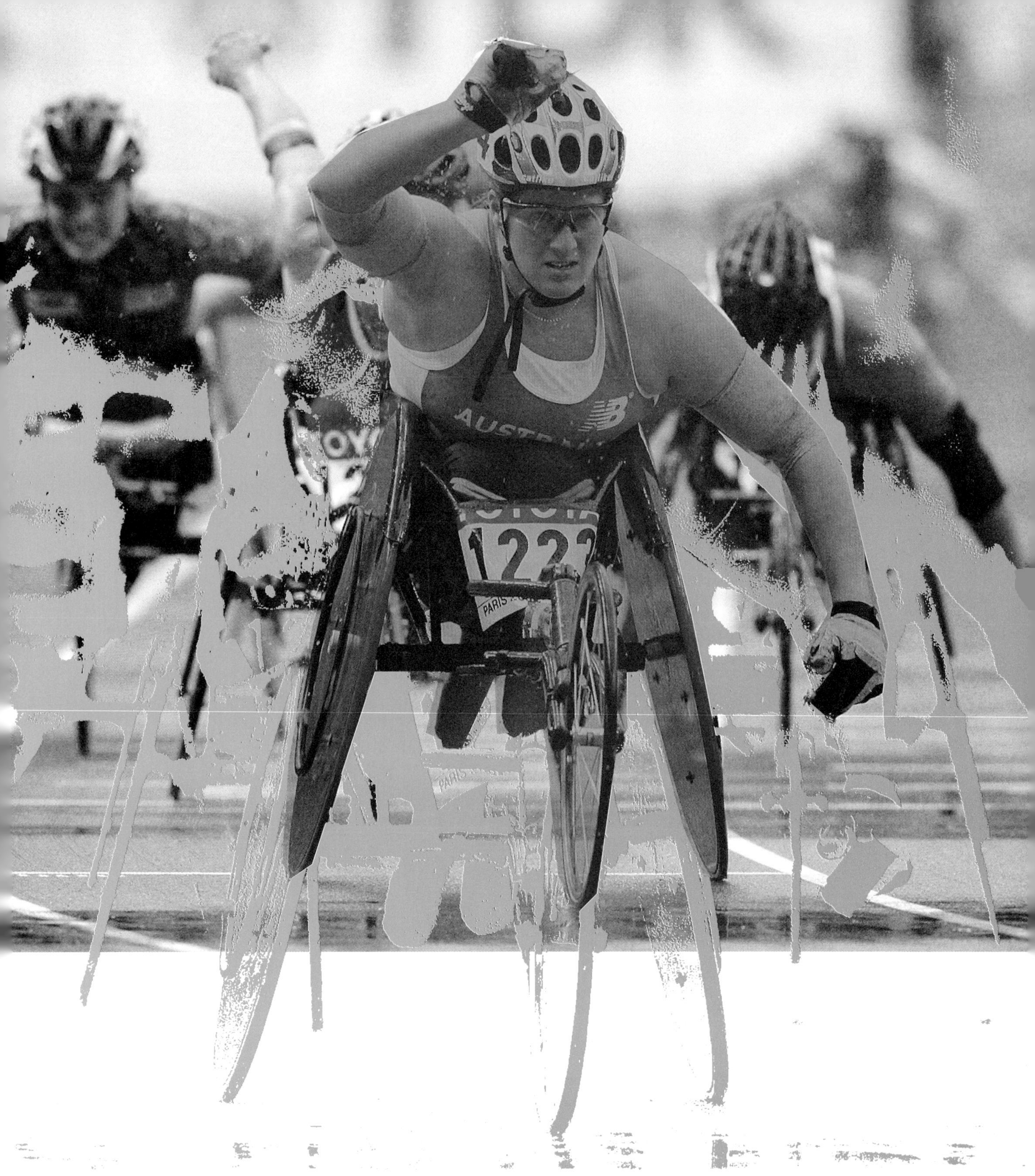

No matter what happens you can cope

AN ACTION PLAN FOR ENTERING THE SPECIAL WORLD

- When confronted with a new situation, take time to weigh it up.
- Ask for help if you feel unsure.
- Make sure what you are about to do is not dangerous.
- Make sure you trust all the people involved.
- Have the courage to take the first step.
- Just because you don't like something doesn't mean it's not worth doing.
- Don't make excuses along the way.
- Make sure you learn before you quit.
- Don't expect the journey to be fair.

In life we are often confronted with the following things:

- Sometimes we get teased at school
- Sometimes we lose something very valuable
- Sometimes our pets die
- Sometimes we break bones
- Sometimes we get into trouble
- Sometimes we fail tests
- Sometimes we miss goals
- Sometimes we don't get chosen for sports teams
- Sometimes we are not allowed out late at night
- Sometimes we forget to do homework
- Sometimes we get lost
- Sometimes we see our grandparents get old
- Sometimes a close relative dies
- Sometimes our parents separate
- Sometimes we get sick and have to go to hospital
- Sometimes we have to wear clothes we hate.

When these things happen, we might feel like we can't cope. But then we find ourselves in a new world, where we discover something amazing about ourselves:

No matter what happens ... WE CAN COPE

Whenever you are faced with a situation which scares you, just keep saying to yourself, 'I can COPE. I can COPE. I can COPE. I can COPE ...'

Start solving the problem, and remember, a big part of coping is to get help when you need it.

When you feel like saying 'I can't', add the word 'yet' at the end: 'I can't cope ... yet.' This way you'll know that one day 'I can't' will become 'I can'. I remember saying to my dad after falling off my bike, 'I can't do it,' but you know what? He knew I would one day, so he kept encouraging me to keep on trying, until finally I did learn to ride without falling off.

HARRY'S STORY

'When my dad lost his job, we had to move to a new state. I was in Grade 4 and all my friends were at my old school. I had been going really well at the cricket club and had just got into the As. And I had set my room up at home just the way I liked it.

When Dad said we had to move, I was mad, because it wasn't fair. I kept saying he should get a job in Melbourne and not in Brisbane.

I hated the move at first. I had no friends and didn't know anyone, and we weren't near a cricket ground.

After about a week in our new place, my dad took me for a walk on the beach and told me how hard it was for him to start his new job and how he needed me for support. He said he didn't know anyone, and his job meant he had to do new stuff he hadn't done before. I told him I felt the same. I missed my friends and I wanted to go home.

I will always remember my dad just looking at me and saying, 'Well, you can't go home. I couldn't make it here without you.'

From then on, for some reason I managed to cope, and things got better. I'm not saying it was easy, but I did cope.'

You Have Control Over Your Life

While this chapter has talked a lot about the potential for bad things to happen, there is a light at the end of the tunnel. **Most of the time life is good! In fact, life is great!**

You are an amazing, strong, talented person who can try to be anything you want to be. Sure, there will be disappointments along the way, but for every disappointment there will also be a dozen great opportunities. And the only way to find them out is to start flying ... Right NOW!

HERO:
IAN THORPE

Ian Thorpe's journey into the special world came at a very young age. At just 14, Ian became the youngest ever male swimmer to be named in the Australian team.

Ian has gone on to establish himself as one of the greatest swimmers of all time. Having broken numerous world records and won multiple Olympic gold and silver medals, Ian has become a role model for young Australians.

Perhaps what is most impressive, however, is the fact that Ian has not lost touch with other areas of his life while developing his swimming career. Along with participating in the special world of an international celebrity, Ian has managed to become one of the most sought-after people in the world to advertise products and events.

Despite Ian's apparently glamorous life, his special world comes at a price. His training starts at 5 am five mornings per week and lasts for two hours. Twice a week he backs this up with an hour of weight training. In the afternoons, Ian swims again for two hours and has only Wednesday mornings and Sundays off.

The special world you choose for yourself will always come at a price. The special world is never easy, and long-term dedication is required to make it through.

It takes a whole village to raise a child.

Finding a Mentor

Everyone needs friends and **mentors** in their life. Mentors are people we can learn from and trust. Sometimes our mentors will be our parents or teachers; sometimes they will be older friends, or brothers or sisters.

When you find a special world you have to enter, it is a great comfort to find a mentor who has been there before you. You would be amazed how many people are willing to help! Have you seen the movie *The Wizard of Oz*? Gilda the Good Witch 'mentors' Dorothy by encouraging her to follow the yellow brick road. Dorothy then meets the Cowardly Lion, the Tin Man and the Scarecrow, who become her best friends and join her quest, helping her find her way home.

FILM:
THE WIZARD OF OZ

The Ordinary World

The Wizard of Oz is a classic story which starts on a small farm in Kansas. The central character, Dorothy, lives with her aunt and uncle and daydreams her way through life, wondering what is over the rainbow.

The Call to Adventure

One day a giant storm hits Kansas and blows Dorothy and her house into another land called Oz.

The Special World

For Dorothy, Oz is the special world. It is here she meets Gilda, the Good Witch of the North, who tells Dorothy that her house has landed right on top of the Wicked Witch of the East and killed her, thus freeing all the munchkins who were under the witch's control. Gilda gives Dorothy a magic pair of slippers to thank her for freeing the munchkins. But little do Dorothy and Gilda know, the Wicked Witch of the West is already plotting to take the slippers back and revenge her sister's death.

Allies and Enemies

To get home, Dorothy is told she must walk the yellow brick road to the Emerald City. Along the way, Dorothy meets several companions: a Scarecrow, who wishes he had brains, a Tin Man, who wishes he had a heart, and a Lion, who wishes he could find his courage.

Together with Dorothy's dog, Toto, they set off for the city.

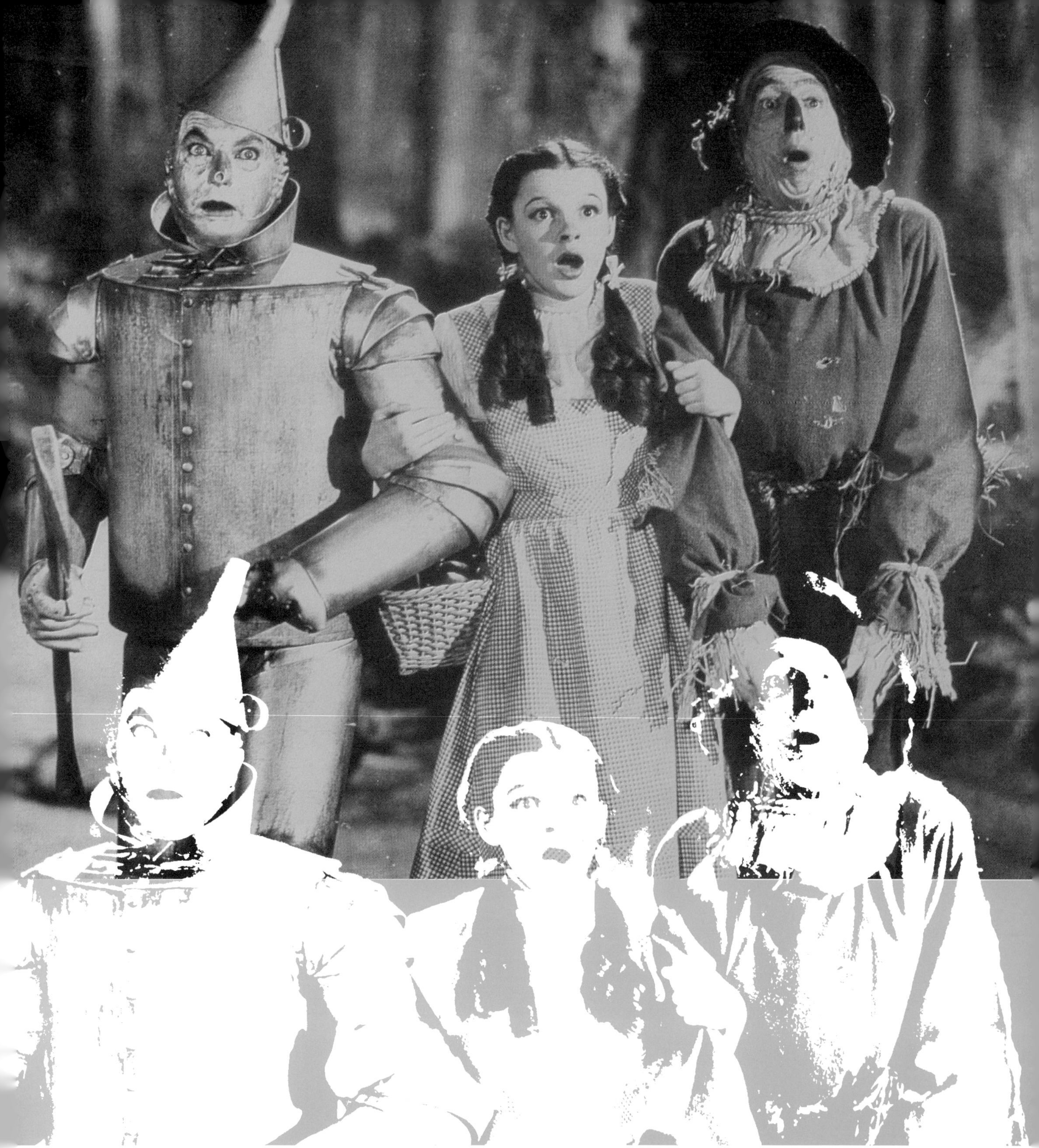

Tests and Challenges

When they finally reach the Emerald City, Dorothy and her friends are given the task of defeating the Wicked Witch of the West and returning with her broomstick if they are to get their wishes.

They visit the enchanted forest and face the witch and her army of winged monkeys. Dorothy is captured and her friends must overcome their fears to save her.

Slaying the Dragon

In the end, all three of Dorothy's friends overcome their weaknesses to help Dorothy escape. In the process, they discover that they do not need anyone to grant their wishes after all, because they have each found what they were looking for within themselves during their journey.

The Reward

Dorothy finally returns to Kansas when she discovers that she also had the power within her all along. By clicking her heels three times and saying the words, 'There is no place like home,' Dorothy and her dog Toto are returned safely to Kansas.

SUMMARY: THE SPECIAL WORLD

- *The special world is a place from which you cannot easily return*
- *The journey begins with just one step*
- *The special world can be both a positive and negative place*
- *Accept or reject the journey*
- *To accept the journey you must take responsibility and not ...*
  - *justify your progress*
  - *ignore the truth*
  - *deny what is happening to you*
  - *blame others for your misfortune*
  - *give up first time*
  - *cling to a victim mentality*
- *Mentors can help you enter the special world*
- *Your destiny is in your own hands*

Allies and enemies

You have forgotten who you are, and so have forgotten me. Look inside yourself, Simba. You are more than what you have become.

THE LION KING

4 CHAPTER FOUR

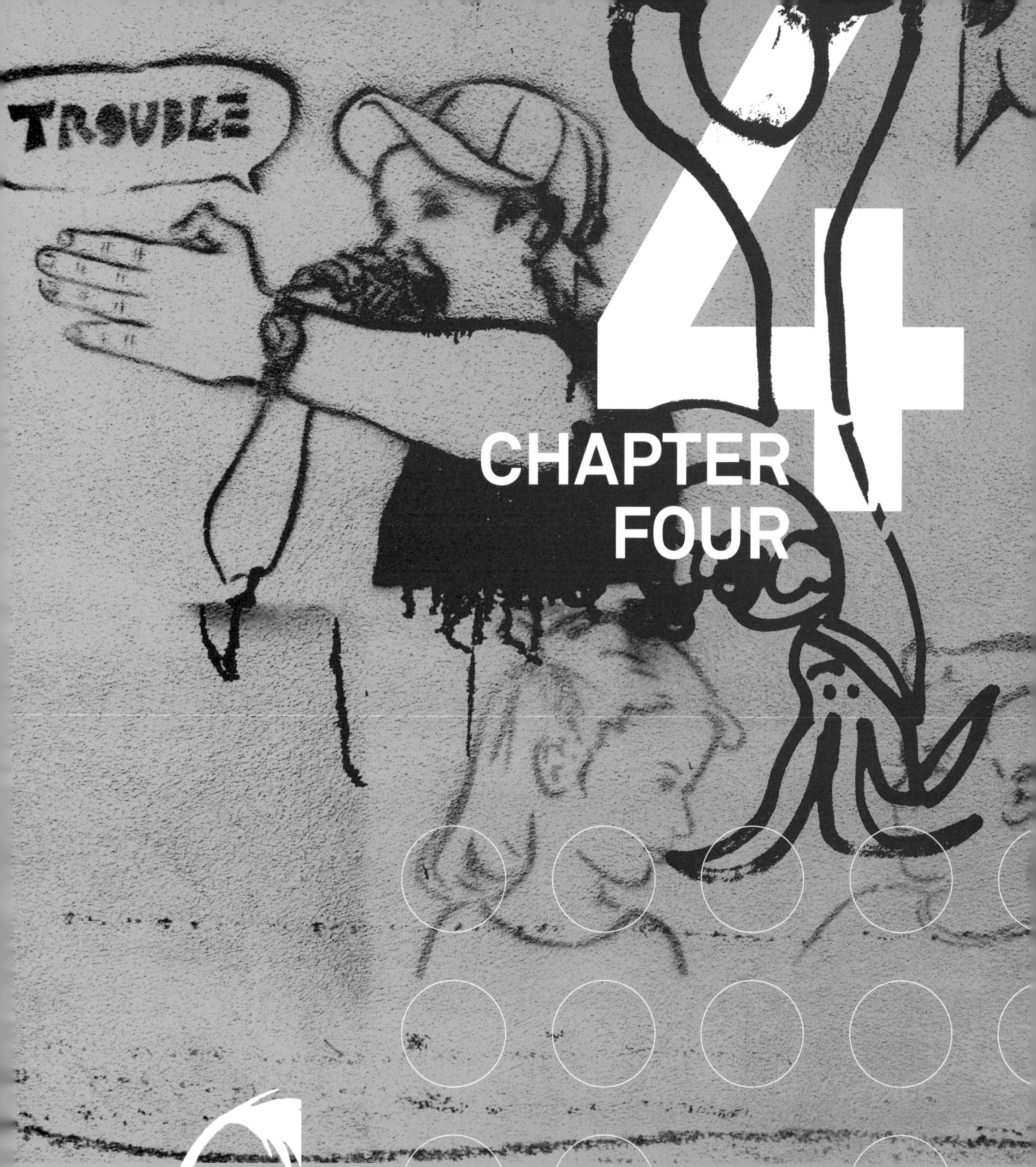
TROUBLE

Allies are good friends and people who we learn to trust over a period of time. Sometimes they can help us along the way in our journey through the special world. Sometimes people start out as allies but turn into enemies, or we think they are enemies but they turn out to be friends.

In the schoolyard, all sorts of groups form. Some days people are your friends, and then other days the same people aren't. While this is all a part of growing up, being mean to your friends is a good habit to break as early as you can.

• Friends do not talk behind each other's backs.

• Friends don't put you down to make themselves feel good.

• Friends don't exclude you from the group.

Sadly, there will always be people who don't treat their friends well, and the chances are that somewhere along the way we have all done one or all of the things listed above. Our journey is not about being perfect, but it is about trying to do our best. Being our best is not something that can happen some of the time — it needs a continual effort, and keeping up that effort is hard work!

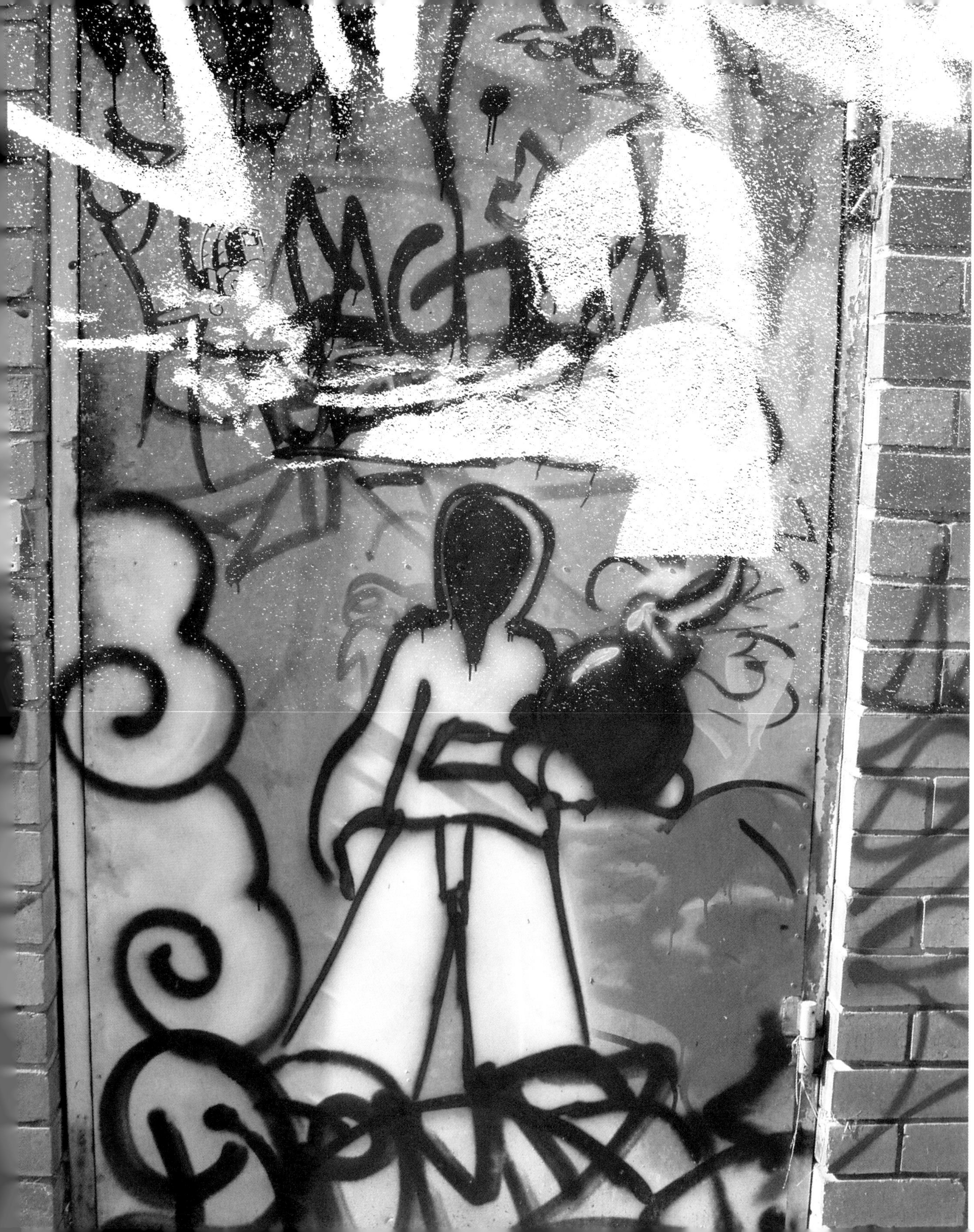

What Is Right and What Is Wrong?

Deciding what is right and what is wrong takes time and patience. However there are a number of very good rules which can help you decide.

These include:

Be kind

Is this action going to hurt anyone?

Do unto others as you would have done unto you

How would you feel if this was done to you?

Assume the world is watching

Would you still do this thing if everyone you knew could see you do it?

When people are picking on you, it is easy to talk about them behind their backs. When people put us down, our natural instinct is to put them down in return. But as our journey goes on, we develop the character required not to do these things.

It's a bit like Frodo in *The Lord of the Rings*. He has many friends and enemies who try to trick him and mislead him, and it would have been very easy for him to slip on the ring and become all-powerful. But that's the one thing he mustn't do if he is to save everyone else. It takes character not to take the easy way out.

Just as sometimes at school or at home, it takes character to be picked on and not to pick back.

Stand up for Yourself

Of course, not picking on others does not mean you cannot stand up for yourself or for others. Despite what your teachers and parents will tell you, sometimes there is no option but to fight for what you believe in. But as we will see below, there are many ways to fight without being violent.

One of the biggest tests in life is being bullied. It can be an awful and lonely experience. But there are some things you can do to try and take control.

DEALING WITH BULLIES

- Ignore what the bully has to say. After all, they are just words.
- Tell a teacher straight away, before the bullying is out of control.
- Tell your friends and ask for help.
- Talk to your parents.
- Keep telling people until the problem is addressed.
- Try not to be alone in the playground – hang out with your friends and people you can trust.
- Stay clear of the bully.
- If you are bullied by a group, try to confront the weakest member in the group.
- Always keep eye contact with a bully, then turn and walk away.
- If you cannot walk away, just repeat everything the bully says to you.
- If you are good at humour, use it.
- Keep telling yourself you can cope.
- Believe in yourself, not the bully.
- Stand tall and strong, even if you don't feel it, and walk with confidence.
- Do self-defence training classes.
- Write down everything that happens to you and when it happens.

Being bullied is not your fault. If you need help, GET IT. There is far more strength in asking for help when you need it than there is in trying to ignore a problem which won't go away. Involve teachers and parents and make sure you don't hide it away. People may appear to call you a dobber for this, but deep inside they are glad someone is finally doing something about the situation.

If people are constantly hurting you physically and no one is doing anything about it, stand up to them.

At heart, bullies are cowards. They never pick on people stronger than them – you becoming the victim is what they want.

BE stronger. More often than not bullies back down. If they don't back down, then get your friends together to help you as a group.

Sometimes the bullying might get to you. Find a safe place and/or people you can trust to let out your feelings and emotions. Sometimes when we are being bullied for being different, it is really hard to fit in with other people. Remember that we are all different, and it is this difference which makes us special.

When someone tries to hurt you ...

When someone calls you a name or does something to try to hurt you, imagine it's coming at you like a slow cricket ball delivery, and you are at the crease at a big cricket stadium, and you hit it for six out of the ground. Visualise this in your mind each time someone calls you a name or hurts you, until the ball disappears over the stands. If you do this in your mind each time, then it can't hurt you, because you didn't allow it to get into your body or mind.

You might have a better way to visualise this — maybe an invisible protective bubble around you that disintegrates insults! Use whatever works for you. But remember, the mind is a very powerful tool, and when you master it, it will be your greatest ally.

'Trust in the force, Luke'.
OBI-WAN KENOBI, STAR WARS

MICHELLE'S STORY

'Every day I hated going to school. There was this group of four girls who made my life a misery. They would wait for me in the morning and take my money, and if I didn't give it to them they would tease me all day.

I figured it was better to give them money than to get teased, so I did. But it didn't stop there. At recess they would walk behind me and trip me up by kicking my heels. It used to make me so mad and frustrated I would cry, and then they would tease me for being a sook.

At lunchtime I used to go to the library just to get away from them. One day I was sitting in between the rows of books when our PE teacher came up to me and asked what the problem was. I said I didn't want to say, but after a while I told him. I couldn't believe he was not surprised. It seems these girls had been picking on lots of people.

Eventually I told the principal and one of the girls was suspended. When this happened the others hated me even more, but by now I had joined the netball group at school and spent my lunchtimes in the gym. I made some friends there and walked to school with them, and even though the other girls still hated me, they never asked me for money again.'

The Courage of Your Convictions

To stand up to the enemies you will meet along life's journey, it really helps if:

- You understand who you are
- You understand what your purpose is
- You understand the principles which apply to your journey.

If these three things are in place, you will find a renewed capacity to face your enemies.

Enemies, of course, can come in many shapes and sizes. Often they are people, sometimes they are emotions such as doubt or anger.

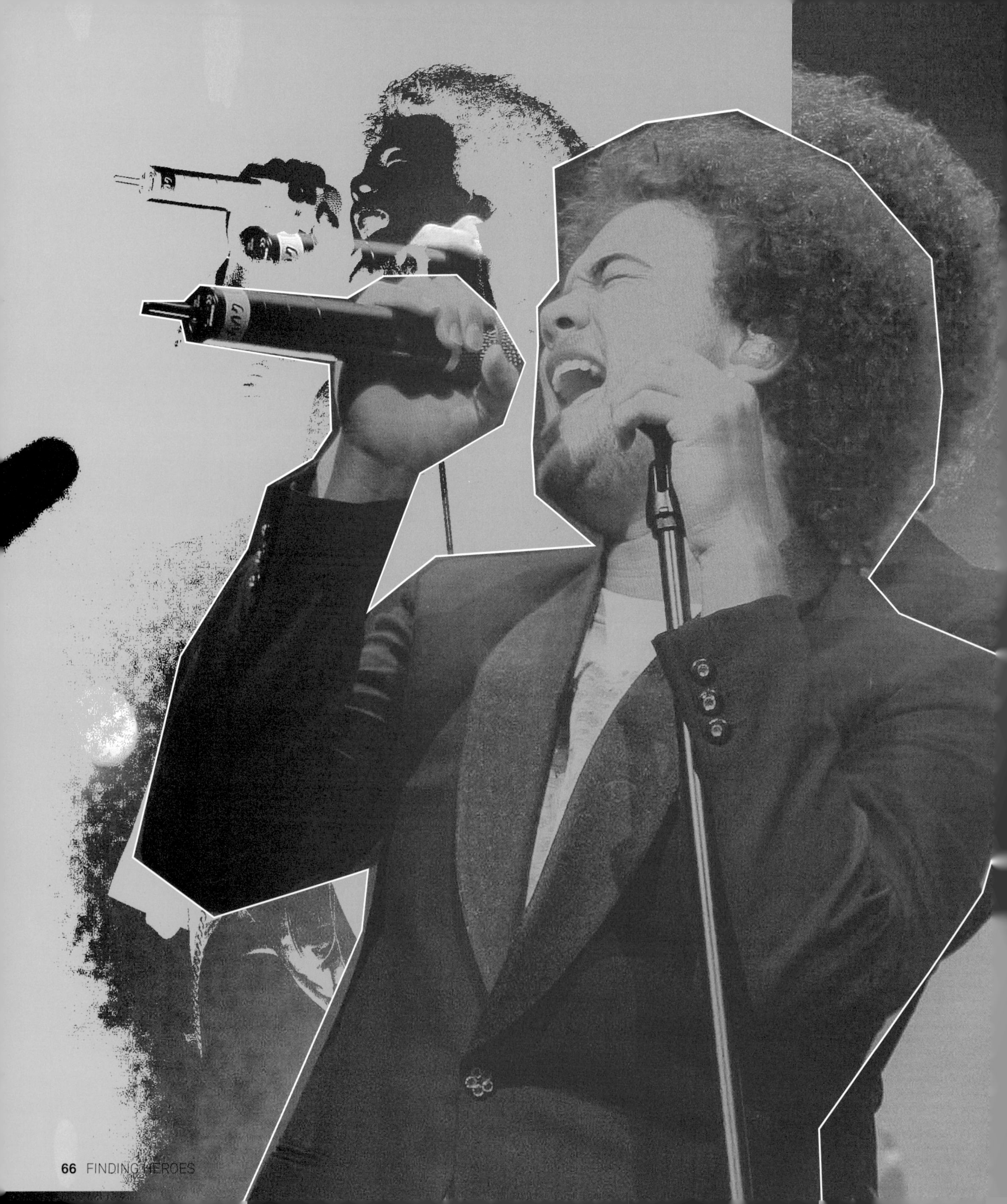

HERO:
GUY SEBASTIAN

Singer Guy Sebastian found fame on the television show *Australian Idol*. Not only is Guy a great singer, he also stands up for the things he believes in. While many his age might go off the rails after winning a show like *Australian Idol*, Guy has chosen to stay true to the things he believes in.

'It just seems like you have to do that to be cool now, and I want to be different. I choose the way I am, and it's very difficult and you get slagged off a lot. But that's me and I'm not changing.'

Learn to be Assertive, NOT Aggressive or Passive.

Learning to stand up for ourselves does not mean we have to be aggressive. It just means we have to be **assertive**. Being assertive means being clear and direct about what we want.

Assertiveness comes with confidence, and confidence comes with experience. That's why it is important to leave your 'comfort zone' as often as possible and try new things.

If we lose our temper often, we find that other people are controlling us. Losing your temper is giving away your power to someone else. If we are simply passive and let people walk all over us, we often find that we are concentrating on our negative points too often and not enough on our positive points.

Learn to say NO. Learn to take control of your own life.

YOU are your own best ally. It is often our own self-belief which will be our strongest guiding force. Our self-belief helps us understand the difference between right and wrong, and good and evil. Self-belief and understanding will also help us decide who are our friends and who are our enemies.

Like Simba who looks to his father for strength and instead finds himself, so we too can discover the unknown strength inside us. All we have to do is test ourselves and look!

CRAIG STEVENS

After Ian Thorpe was disqualified from the qualifying trials for the Athens Olympics for a false start, his swimming partner Craig Stevens decided to step aside to allow Thorpe — the undisputed world champion in the 400-metre freestyle event — to compete in his place.

It took a superhuman effort for Ian Thorpe to get back on the blocks and win the final at the Olympics. But he owed it to Craig Stevens to control his negative thoughts and 'pay back' his friend. Before the event, Thorpe said:

```
'I'm excited about swimming the event
and not worried about the pressure …
I don't want to be cautious about it
at all.'
```

This event shows what friends are really all about. Craig Stevens had every right to swim in the 400 metres, and Ian Thorpe had every right to complain about missing out even though he was world and Olympic champion. Instead, both of them looked inside themselves and made difficult decisions. Fortunately they both had the mental, physical and emotional character to overcome the odds and do the 'right thing'.

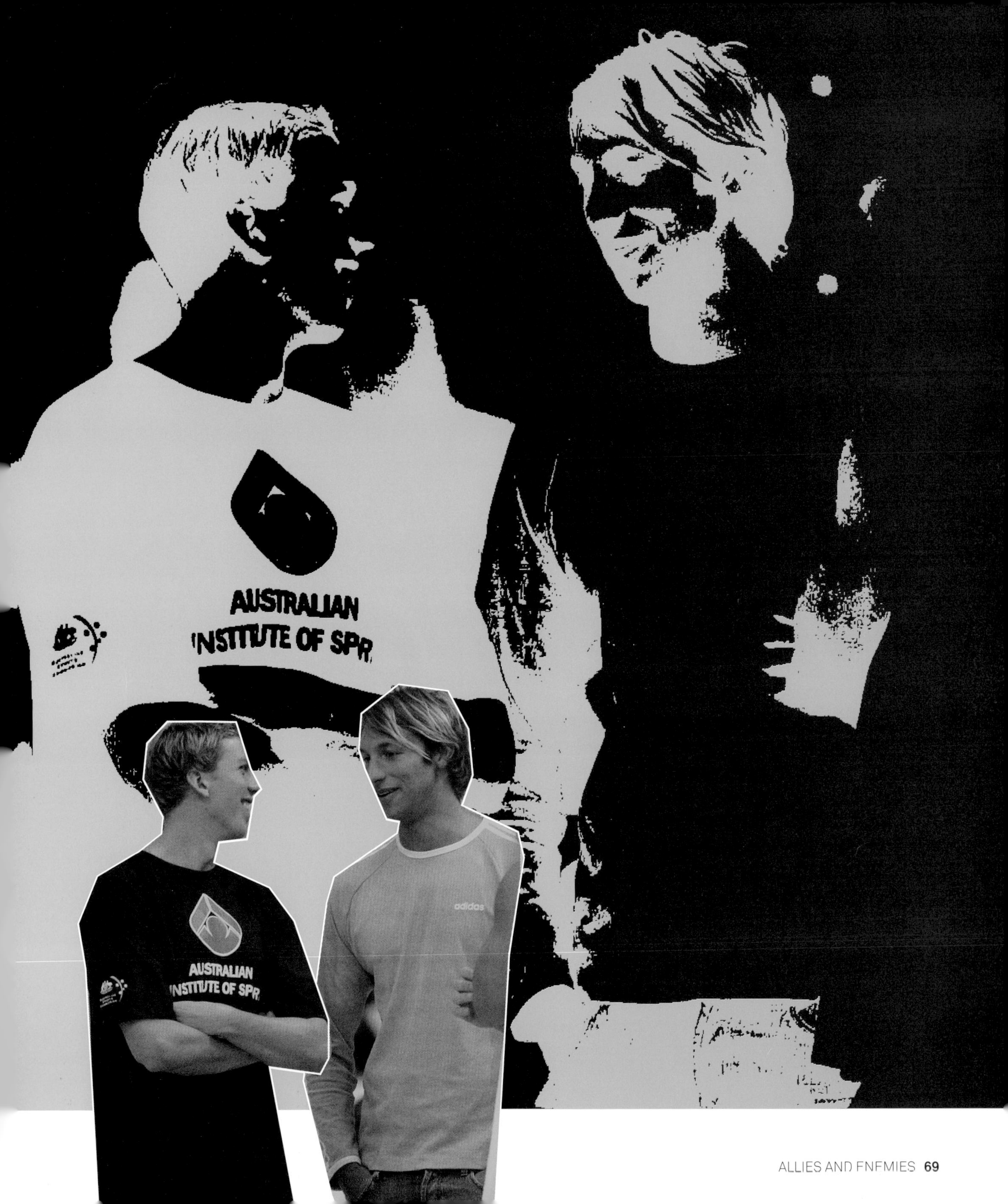
AUSTRALIAN
INSTITUTE OF SPR
AUSTRALIAN
INSTITUTE OF SPR
adidas

Think outside the square

One of the problems with school is that it often focusses too much on schoolwork and not enough on other stuff. Recently, researchers have discovered that people can be smart in more areas than one.

For example, if we were asked to 'show' who we are, we might try a number of different ways to do it.

We could draw it
We could paint it
We could dance it
We could sing it
We could explain it
We could act it
We could write it
We could build it
We could even dream it!

In other words, there are many ways to express yourself and gain self-esteem, and different people are 'intelligent' in different ways. Part of our journey is to discover which ones suit us best.

The reality of life is that not all of us can be winners at everything we do. But just because we do not succeed at one thing does not mean we are unable to succeed at others. Sadly, some of us allow ourselves to get less and less confident as we keep trying new things and 'failing'.

We begin to believe we are no good or hopeless at stuff, and we forget all the things we can be good at:

- I can be a good friend
- I can be a good student
- I can be helpful to others
- I can keep score if I don't want to play
- I can work backstage or do make-up if I don't want to act
- I can play guitar if I don't want to sing
- I can become cox if I don't want to row.

There are always options in life.

THE LION KING

The Ordinary World

Simba is born into an ordinary world where he is the son of the great king Mufasa. As the son of a king he is free to roam the pride lands without fear of being hurt.

The Call to Adventure

Simba's call to adventure comes when his father is killed and his evil uncle Scar blames Simba and sets about taking over the kingdom.

The Special World

Believing he was responsible for his father's death, Simba runs away through the elephant graveyard into exile, and into a journey of self discovery.

Allies and Enemies

His main enemy is his uncle Scar, with his band of hyenas. After running away, Simba is adopted by two friends named Pumbaa and Timon who help raise him, until one day he bumps into a lioness named Nala who he was once best friends with. Nala, along with an old ape named Rafiki encourage him to return to the pride lands and defeat his uncle Scar.

Test and Challenges

Simba's greatest test is to overcome his own fear and live up to the memory of his father. He does this after his father appears to him in a vision.

Slaying the Dragon

Simba returns to face Scar and the hyenas. In a great battle, Simba and his friends defeat Scar and the hyenas.

The Reward

Simba's reward is to take his rightful place as the king of the pride lands. With Nala by his side, he becomes the ruler of his lands. Most importantly, he rediscovers who he really is.

SUMMARY: ALLIES AND ENEMIES

- *Be a good friend*
- *Stand up for yourself*
- *Get help when you need it*
- *Being yourself is cool*
- *Be assertive, not aggressive or passive*
- *Take control of your life*
- *You are your own best ally*
- *Self-expression takes many forms*
- *Think outside the square*

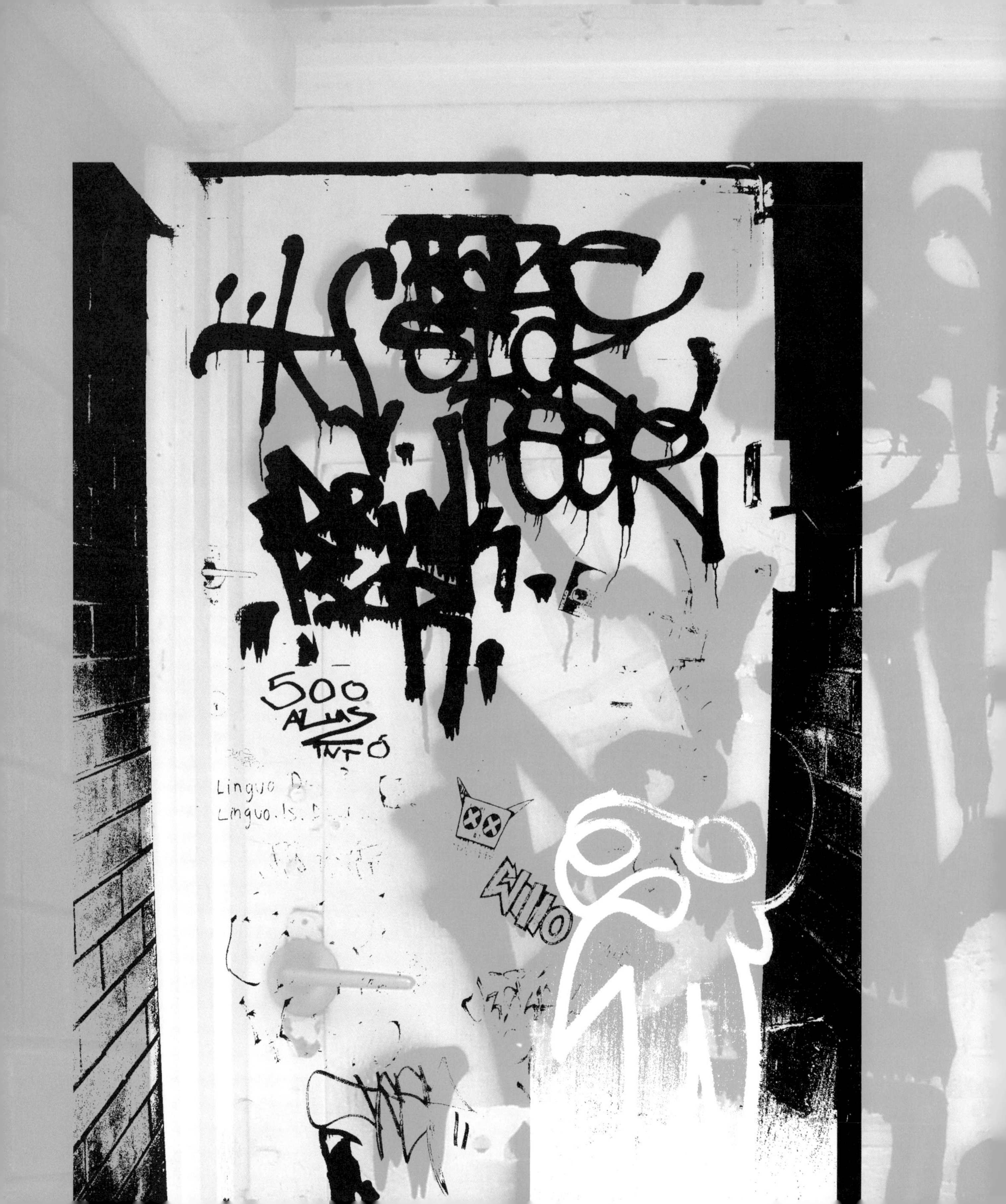
500

5

TESTS AND CHALLENGES

It does not do to dwell on dreams, Harry, and forget to live.

HARRY POTTER AND THE PHILOSOPHER'S STONE

Tests and Challenges

If your journey through the special world is worth taking and your destination is worth reaching, then you will face many, many tests and challenges along the way. But the only time to be afraid is when you are not honest with yourself.

Most people living in the ordinary world look at the lives of successful people and ask, how can they be so amazing? The answer is simple ... they are not amazing. They are just ordinary people on extraordinary journeys who have faced and overcome their own tests and challenges.

HERO: NELSON MANDELA

'Our deepest fear is not that we are inadequate.

Our deepest fear is that we are powerful beyond measure.

It is our light, not our darkness, which frightens us.

We ask ourselves: who am I to be brilliant, gorgeous, talented, fabulous?

Actually, who are you not to be?

Your playing small doesn't serve the world.

There is nothing enlightened about shrinking so that other people won't feel insecure around you.

We were born to manifest the glory that is within us.

It is not just within some of us; it is in everyone.

And when we let our light shine, we unconsciously give other people permission to do the same.

As we are liberated from our fear, our presence automatically liberates others.'

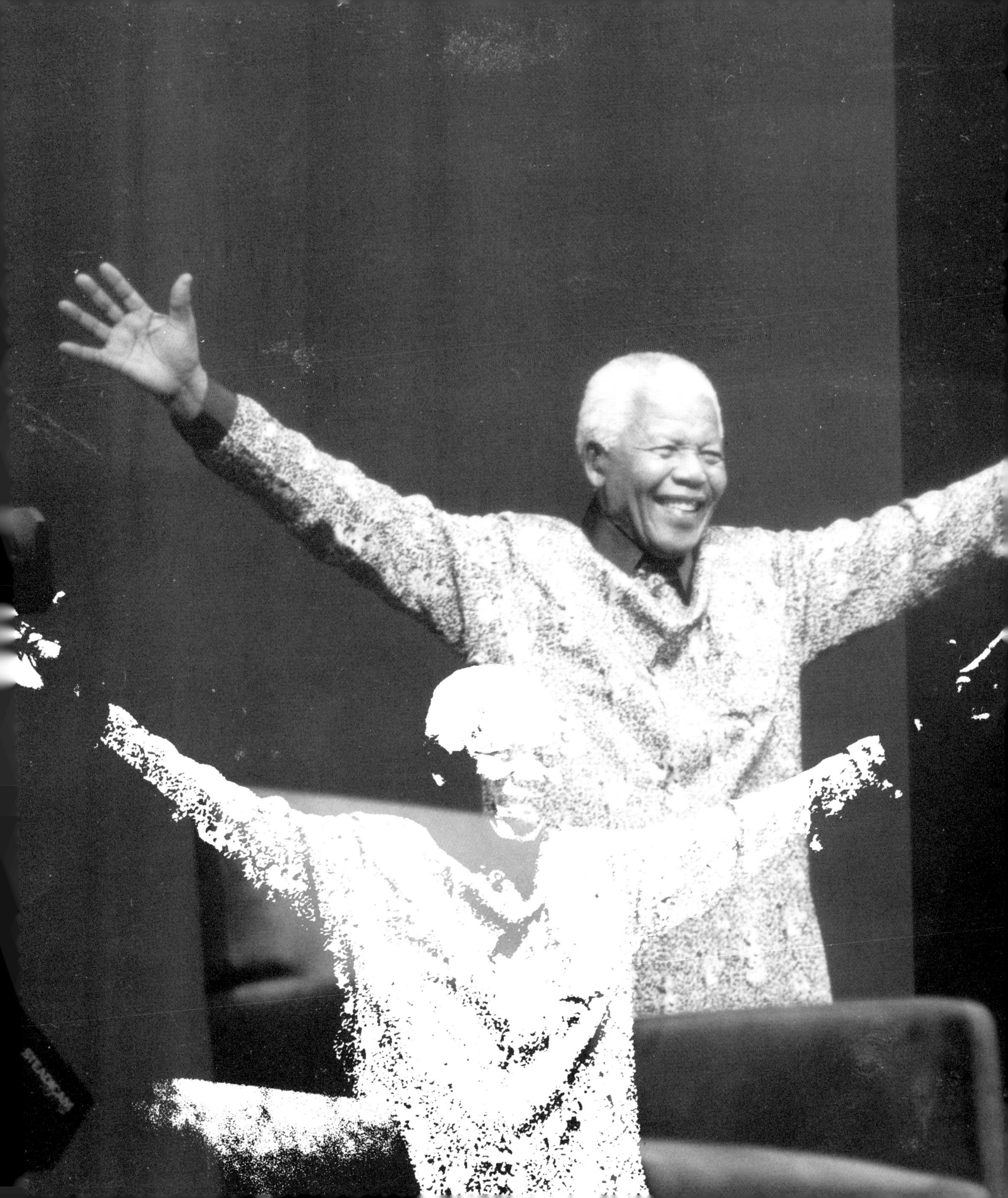

There Is Always a Choice

No matter how bad a situation might seem, it is an important lesson in life to understand that we always have a choice.

Sometimes the choices are very clear and other times they are really hard to make. Sometimes it seems like we don't have any choice at all.

For example, sometimes your parents might not let you go out until you have cleaned your room. They tell you that you have no choice: if you do not clean your room, you will not be allowed out.

There is always a choice ... it just might not be obvious!

But in fact you have lots of choices:

- You could clean your room and go out.
- You could not clean your room, and not go out.
- You could sneak out without telling them.
- You could pay your little sister to clean your room.
- You could pretend to clean your room while listening to CDs instead.

The list of choices is endless ...

You Are in Control

Once you accept that there is always a choice, you accept that **you are in control**, even when you don't feel you are. When our parents send us off to our room, we definitely don't feel in control. When we are picked on at school, we often don't feel in control. The trick here is to practise being in control.

Next time your parents send you to your room, as you walk down the corridor keep saying to yourself, 'My parents are sending me, but I am in control.'

The next time you get picked on at school, keep telling yourself, 'This person may be teasing me, but I control whether they hurt me or not.'

Choices do have consequences. But once we overcome the fear of making choices, we begin to discover that we **are** in control. Like Harry when he went to the mirror searching for happiness, we learn to take control for ourselves. Harry had no choice in his parents dying, but he did have a choice about how he coped. Despite the bad things which had happened to him, Harry made the choice to look forwards rather than backwards.

Get Used to Tests and Challenges

If you have read the Harry Potter books or seen the movies, you will understand the huge number of choices Harry has to make. What we also learn is that Harry keeps getting challenged.

Just as you overcome one challenge, another seems to come along.

Here are some of the challenges faced by Harry, and also a list of challenges you may have faced in your life:

Harry Potter

- Harry has to fit into a new school
- Harry gets picked on a bit
- Harry has to discover new friends
- He has to learn to play quidditch
- He has to trap the winged Snitch
- He has to face the three-headed dog
- He has to pass the sleeping troll
- He sees his parents in the Mirror of Erised

You

- Have you ever been to a new school?
- Have you ever been picked on?
- Have you ever had to make new friends?
- Have you ever played a new sport?
- Have you ever tried to catch something?
- Have you ever faced a scary animal?
- Have you ever met scary people?
- Have you ever lost a family member?

There are no short cuts in life.

DANIEL'S STORY

'When I was six, my parents got divorced. I stayed in our house living with my mum, but I really miss my dad.

He lives with another lady and my mum doesn't like her, so I feel guilty whenever I visit. Dad is always trying to do fun stuff, but it is not the same without my real mum there. I get a lot of attention from him now and from Mum too, but it didn't used to be like that. They always used to fight.

I know I have choices now. I want to get on with my dad's new girlfriend even if Mum doesn't. I wish they would get back together.'

Control What You Can

Like many of us, Daniel comes from a broken home. When this happens, kids have to grow up fast. It can be really hard. Here are some things to remember:

- What happened is not your fault.
- You can still love Mum and Dad the same even if they don't still love each other.
- You can try to accept the new friends Mum and Dad have, but you don't have to love them the same.
- You can always talk to someone outside your family if you need help.

Keep Going

Life is great fun if you give it a go. And sometimes it doesn't work out. So what?

Mountain climbers face challenges all the time. Sometimes they go on. Sometimes they stop.

When the going gets tough, the tough get going.

HERO
BRIGITTE MUIR

It took her four attempts and 39 years to do it, but on 27 May 1997, Brigitte Muir became the first Australian female to reach the top of Mount Everest. Her hero's journey began in the tiny town of Natimuk in the Wimmera, and ended at the highest point in the world.

Along the way she had climbed the highest mountains on seven continents, and during preparation in 1996 she had been involved in a fatal expedition, cut short by a snowstorm which killed 11 other climbers.

According to her then husband, Jon Muir, Brigitte's greatest asset is her mental and emotional strength:

'Most men have got no idea what true strength is. They think they've got it, muscles and so on. That is a small part of strength.'

In the end it was Brigitte's spirit which took her to the top of Everest. As Jon again points out:

'What is worthwhile in life? I think it is worth living and dreaming. If you don't you may be dead anyhow – inside.

It may not be easy, life isn't easy, but dreams keep you alive.'

Think Positive Thoughts

No matter how bad a situation might be, there are always positives to be found. They might seem like small things at first, but the more you think about them, the more positive they become.

Negative Thought

- I hate maths
- I'm sad mum and dad split up
- My sister gets all the attention
- My friends all have the latest clothes

Positive Possibility

- I can pass something even when I hate it
- I can cope when I get sad. If I can cope with this, I can cope with anything!
- I can learn not to depend on attention
- I can be cool in old clothes

Try a few positive possibilities for yourself.

HERO: LLEYTON HEWITT

Famous athletes often talk about an inner voice which tells them to keep going when they are tired.

Here, Lleyton Hewitt talks about being able to control your mind when faced with big challenges:

'Sometimes I think, you know, you're not human if [a negative voice] doesn't a little bit enter your mind now and then.

I think the quicker you're able to block it out and get on with the next point, then the better off you're going to be.

So that's something that I've tried to work on since being a junior, basically, trying to block out the negative thoughts.'

Learning to control your mind and think positive thoughts is a big part of the journey through the special world.

Getting Along with Family

Just growing up as part of a family can be a real test and a challenge of life's journey.

Here are a few questions to talk over with your mum or dad:

- What would you do if I decided to follow a career as a singer and wanted to drop out of school?
- Can we read through some of your old school reports and see how well you did?
- If I ever get into trouble and you're not there, what should I do?
- If I have a problem I don't feel I can talk to you about, who should I talk to?
- Tell me about a few times you made mistakes.
- Tell me about a few times you did something you should not have done.

HERO:
BRITNEY SPEARS

Whether you like her music or not, Britney Spears has led an amazing life, and she puts it down to her relationship with her mother:

'The older I get, the more I realize that. Growing up, I knew so many girls who used to fight all the time with their moms – over everything, it seemed: boys, clothes, curfews – and that used to make me so sad. I wished they could all have a mom like mine.'

This has to go both ways of course. Britney's mother has faith in her too:

'Kids will make mistakes; they'll do things they shouldn't. That's a given. But didn't we all make mistakes when we were younger? I always try to remind myself of that and stay as open-minded as possible.'

HARRY POTTER AND THE PHILOSOPHER'S STONE

The Ordinary World

Harry Potter is an orphan who lives with the Dursley family. Harry's parents were killed by the evil wizard Voldemort. Harry isn't happy living with the Dursleys who don't treat him very well.

The Call to Adventure

At the age of 11, Harry receives an invitation to attend Hogwarts School of Witchcraft and Wizardry. Assisted by the giant gamekeeper Hagrid, Harry is decked out with the latest wizard gear.

The Special World

Right from the moment Harry finds himself at the station on platform nine and three quarters, waiting for the train to Hogwarts, Harry is transported into a special world where he is no longer just an ordinary boy. Instead he begins to discover his amazing powers and learns how to use them.

Allies and Enemies

At Hogwarts Harry meets his two best friends, Ron Weasley and Hermione Granger, who, like Harry, are placed into Gryffindor House. Harry's main enemy, Draco Malfoy, is placed in Slytherin, which is run by the wizard Snape who once taught Voldemort.

Tests and Challenges

While there are many tests and challenges to come, first Harry and his friends must avoid the bully Draco. In the process of avoiding Draco, Harry and his friends come face to face with the local troll. They must also face Fluffy, the three-headed dog, as they continue on their quest to find the philosopher's stone.

Slaying the Dragon

For Harry, however, the real challenge comes when he discovers a mirror which shows the hopes and dreams of all who look into it. Harry sees his family in the mirror, but it is not until he manages to look into the mirror and see himself that Harry realises he already has everything he needs to live his dreams.

The Reward

In the end, Harry manages to save the philosopher's stone from Voldemort, and because of their bravery, Gryffindor wins the house cup. But most important of all, Harry and his friends have discovered each other, and the friendship is set to grow from there.

Never give in

If you think you're beaten,
you are.

If you think you dare not,
you don't.

If you like to win, but think
you can't,

It is almost certain you won't.

If you think you'll lose,
you're lost,

For out in the world we find

Success begins with your will,

It's all a state of mind.

If you think you're outclassed,
you are.

You've got to think high to rise.

You've got to be sure of
yourself before

You can ever win the prize.

Life's battles don't always go

To the stronger or faster one,

But sooner or later the one
who wins

Is the one who thinks they can.

SUMMARY: TESTS AND CHALLENGES

- *There is always a choice*
- *You are in control*
- *Get used to challenges*
- *Keep going*
- *Think positive thoughts*
- *Get help when you need it*
- *Never give in*

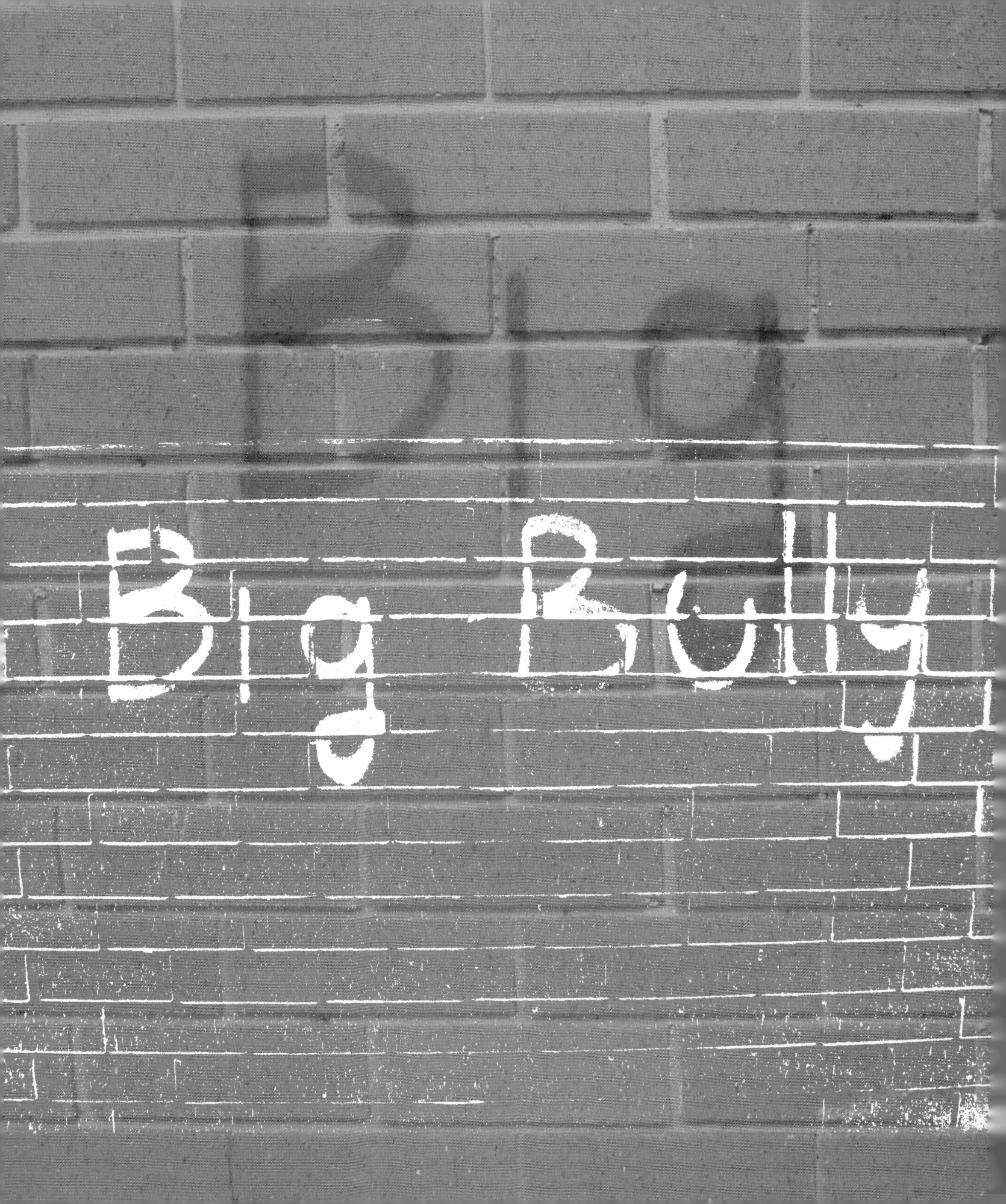
Big
Big Belly

slaying the dragon

There's nothin' wrong with bein' afraid.
Fear's a sensible response to an unfamiliar
situation. Unfamiliar dangerous situation, I
might add. With a dragon that breathes fire
it sure doesn't mean you're a coward if
you're a little scared. SHREK

CHAPTER
SIX 6

Slaying the dragon

In life, we all have to overcome fear at some stage or another. For some of us it is fear of the dark, for others it's fear of performing on stage, for others it is fear of heights. As Donkey says, 'There's nothing wrong with being afraid.' Fear is good. Fear helps us to recognise when things might be dangerous.

On the other hand, fear can also stop us from really having fun and enjoying ourselves. Perhaps the greatest fear worth overcoming is the fear to be yourself. Sometimes we are so scared of what others think of us, we try to do things to impress them rather than being ourselves. But there are many ways you can be yourself and still mix in with a group.

Sometimes we are afraid to be our best, just in case our best isn't as good as other people's. But all you need to be is your best, nothing more. Wanting more is all about ego — wanting to feel better and more important than other people. But ego will not help you enter the cave and fight the dragon!

'To be your best has nothing to do with how many times you win or lose.

It has no relation to where you finish in a race or whether you break world records.

But it does have everything to do with having the vision to dream, the courage to recover from adversity, the determination to never be shifted from your goals.

And the faith to know that whatever the outcome, your greatest competition is not the person standing on the blocks next to you, but yourself.'

Fear can stop us from enjoying ourselves

Learn to Understand Your Fear

Fear is good when it protects us from dangerous situations. Truly courageous people are those who feel fear, but still go ahead and try new stuff anyway.

Do you remember the Athens Olympics in 2004? Hurdler Jana Pittman hurt her knee. Even though running with a sore knee meant she probably would not win the race, she still had the courage to overcome the fear of losing and compete.

This is part of the reason athletes put themselves through so much pain in training. They want to get used to racing when they are gripped by fear. You can do this too. Teaching yourself to overcome the little 'fear voice' inside your head is good practise.

For example, next time you are at the local pool looking up at the 10-metre diving board, instead of fearing the big jump, why not break it down into a series of little jumps?

Start by jumping off the edge of the pool. Next try the starting blocks. After that, try the one-metre board. Then try the five-metre board.

By working your way up to a scary event, you can learn to break fear into little pieces. By the time you get to the end, it doesn't seem as bad.

Here's another example: before you go riding a horse, why not start with a pony?

Learn to Surrender to Fear

Do you remember the *Saddle Club* episode where Lisa had to overcome her fear of cantering? While teaching Lisa to canter, a sudden storm hits, leaving Stevie and Carole stranded on the side of a cliff. Lisa must overcome her fear of cantering and ride for help.

A similar event happened to Donkey in *Shrek* when they were walking over the swing bridge to rescue Princess Fiona. Donkey suddenly froze with fright and turned around to go back. Shrek wasn't happy and started shaking and swinging the bridge. Out of a new fear which distracted his first fear, Donkey started to walk backwards, only to find himself on the other side in no time. He realised he had nothing to be scared of in the first place.

When things like this happen, sometimes we just have to face our fear and go for it!

SARAH'S STORY

'When I was seven, I started horse-riding lessons. I had wanted to ride horses all my life, but when we got to the farm where I was going to try for the first time, I realised how big they really were. Horses don't look that big on television, or even in a paddock, but when you stand right up close to them, they are scary at first.

I can remember putting on my helmet with the other girls. I didn't know anyone and they all seemed so confident. The teacher did not know I was a beginner and I was too embarrassed to tell her, so I tried to climb on the horse she gave me without knowing what I was doing.

As soon as I put my foot in the stirrup, the horse started to move and I was dragged along. Even though it was only walking, my leg was caught and I couldn't get out. I yelled, and this scared the horse which started to run. It dragged me for about five metres before my leg came loose.

Even though I was okay, it took me months before I could get back onto a horse. But this time I did it differently. I started with a new instructor who took things slowly. There were three of us in the group. First we learned to climb onto the saddle while it was mounted on a fence. Once I had the hang of that, she let me try to get on a saddle on a pony. We even walked a bit until I got my confidence. It took three lessons before I got onto a horse. But now I ride them all the time.'

Failure is part of the journey

HERO:
ERNEST SHACKLETON

The famous explorer Ernest Shackleton once placed the following advertisement in a newspaper to try and find a crew for his expedition to Antarctica:

MEN WANTED FOR HAZARDOUS JOURNEY
Small wages, bitter cold, long months of complete darkness, constant danger, safe return doubtful. Honour and recognition in case of success.

Shackleton wanted to become the first person to sail to Antarctica and complete a land crossing of the continent, passing through the South Pole.

He found his crew, and they set off in a ship called the *Endurance*, but they never reached the South Pole. Instead, all 27 men who sailed with him were caught in the pack ice which trapped the ship and then crushed it to pieces. The men managed to get off the ship and, using what supplies they could gather, they survived for months in the freezing cold. When the weather cleared, they made an extremely difficult voyage in three open lifeboats to desolate Elephant Island, where they fought the elements, starvation, boredom and despair before they were finally rescued.

Not one man died, and Shackleton's story is one of the great survival stories. But we still have to ask if it was a failure. After all, they did not achieve what they set out to achieve. What do you think?

Coping with Fear and Failure

We are all scared, and we all fail. These are facts of life. But learning to cope with these facts is also part of life.

When faced with fear or failure, try to ask yourself the following questions:

- What is the worst that can happen?
- What is the most likely outcome?
- What is the best action I can take NOW?
- How can I make this action easier?

In your mind, try making a list of five fears you would like to overcome.

Once you know the answers to these questions, the rest is up to you. It's time for you to take responsibility for your own actions and give things a go.

Words Can Help

Words mould our thoughts. If we use positive words, we tend to develop positive thoughts. While positive thoughts won't help all the time, they can make a difference most of the time.

When we are scared, one of the best things to do is talk to ourselves. Here is an example.

My best friend's mother is very ill and I am scared my own parents may get sick and die.

What is the worst that can happen?

It might come true. My parents might get sick.

What is the most likely outcome?

Most likely my parents will be well and I will have done all this worrying for nothing.

What is the best action I can take now?

The best thing I can do now is comfort my friend. He needs my help.

Sometimes Life IS Tough

Sometimes even when we talk to ourselves and think positively, things still don't really change:

I get picked on every day at school. I hate school and I don't want to go any more.

What is the worst that can happen?

I can keep going to school and keep getting picked on.

What is the most likely outcome?

If I don't do anything about this, they will still pick on me.

But if I stand up to them and get help, it might take time, but the bullying will stop.

What are my options?

I can not go to school.

I can get help.

What is the best action I can take now?

Tell mum or dad or a teacher and get some help.

'But I told Mum and Dad and I told the teacher, and ... My dad said I should punch the biggest kid who picks on me and the others will leave me alone. My mum says if I do this she will never talk to me again. My teacher said she would speak to the bullies and she did. Now they are even madder at me and they pick on me twice as much! When I told the teacher, she said she had done everything she can, and that I should stop complaining because it wasn't that bad.'

If this happens, try going through the questions again ...

What is the worst that can happen?

I keep trying to get help and it only makes it worse.

What is the most likely outcome?

Eventually I will find someone who can help, if I keep trying.

What are my options?

I can give up and let them pick on me.

I can change schools.

I can find someone to help.

I can fight back.

What is the best action I can take now?

Find someone who CAN help.

Life Is Not Always Fair

At other times, life just is not fair. But the questions still help.

I left the gate open yesterday and our new puppy got out. She ran straight onto the road and got hit by a car. I feel so bad because it was all my fault. My dad had to take her to the vet and have her put down.

What is the worst that can happen?

I will feel this way forever. It was all my fault and I will never get over this.

What is the most likely outcome?

With time, I will learn to accept that accidents do happen. They are sad and painful and not fair, but they do happen.

What are my options?

I can keep feeling bad.

I can try to accept that this was just an accident and no one is to blame.

What is the best action I can take now?

Perhaps we could get another puppy, maybe from the RSPCA. Maybe I could save the life of another little dog.

HERO:
CATHY FREEMAN

World and Olympic champion runner Cathy Freeman used pressure to help her win a gold medal in the 400 metres at the Sydney Olympics. With almost 10 million Australians watching her, everyone hoped and expected Cathy would win. She carried this enormous pressure like no other athlete before in our country's history, and when she DID win, it inspired all of us to overcome our own fears and pressures.

But like all heroes' journeys, Cathy's dream started years before it became a reality:

'This has been a dream of mine ever since I was a little girl, and that's why I got really emotional, because this has happened to a little girl like me – an Indigenous Australian.'

Sitting on the track after her stunning win, Cathy said she felt the strength of her mentors and the support of a nation.

'I was just totally overwhelmed. I could feel the crowd totally over me, all around me; I felt everyone's emotions being absorbed into every pore of my body.'

For Cathy, this moment was the reward for her life's work, and her experience is one shared by all those who have managed to overcome fear and live the life of their dreams. Funnily, as is so often the case, the reward has nothing to do with ego:

'I felt so full of gratitude and humility that I clasped my hands in front of me, closed my eyes and said a silent prayer of thanks to God ... I had at last achieved something I'd wanted for so long ... My insides bubbled with happiness. It was a dream come true.'

Slay Your Own Dragons

Allies will help you, but you must slay your own dragons. As Cathy Freeman pointed out at the Sydney Olympics, her friends, family and coaches were all there to support her, but it was Cathy herself who actually had to run the race.

The same will be true for you on your own journey through life. When the moment comes to face your fears, the only person who can overcome them is you. At this point too many people begin to worry about what may happen if they fail.

When this happens, try to change the question around and ask yourself, what will happen if I don't try?

If the answer is worse than what will happen if you fail, then it is time to face up and get moving, time to look inside and realise that the person you thought you were is no match for the one you really are.

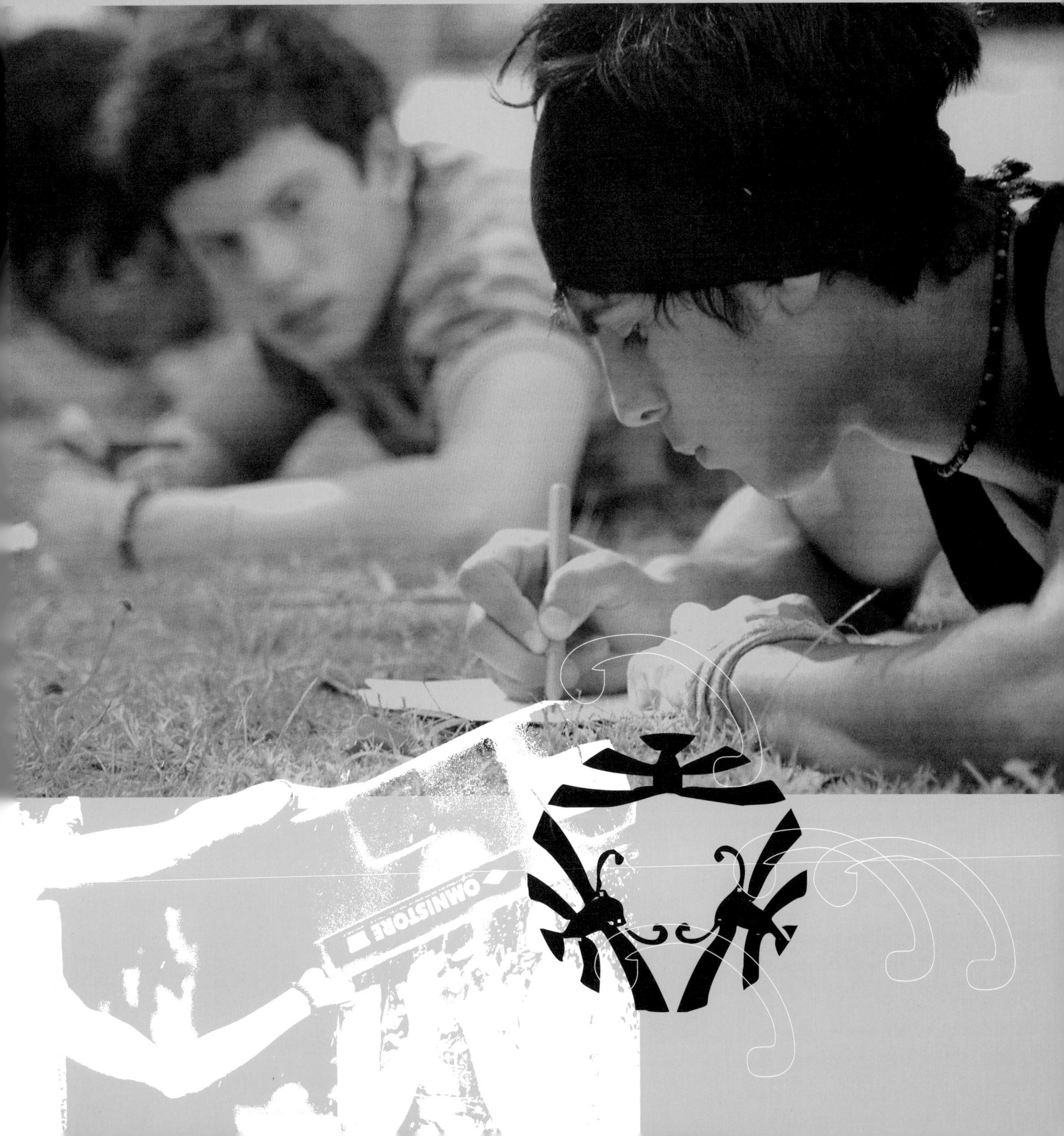
OMNISTORE

Peeling Back the Layers

To find yourself often means trying new things and going on adventures. It's kind of like peeling an onion ...

Shrek:

For your information, there's a lot more to ogres than people think.

Donkey:

Example?

Shrek:

Example? Okay, um, ogres are like onions.

When Shrek talks to Donkey about peeling onions, what he is really saying is that people protect themselves by putting layers around their experiences.

It sounds complex because it is. But a layer is kind of like a suit of armour. You put it on to protect you from arrows and spears in battle. It stops things from getting in. The more layers you have, the greater the protection.

BUT

If you can't take the armour off after the battle, it will continue to stop stuff getting in. It also stops good stuff getting out! Armour is heavy, just like layers can be heavy, so it slows us down. Life is too short to live at half pace when you can go full tilt. Facing fears and peeling back layers allows us to enjoy life fully.

FILM: SHREK

The Ordinary World

Shrek's ordinary world is a swamp on the edge of the kingdom. Shrek lives alone and appears to be happy on the outside, but underneath he would really like to have more friends.

The Call to Adventure

Shrek's call to adventure comes one day when he discovers that Lord Farquaad has banished the fairytale characters into the forest where they move into Shrek's swamp. Shrek feels really uncomfortable about this and goes to confront the Lord. When he arrives, the Lord tells him he can have his swamp back if he can rescue the beautiful Princess Fiona from the Dragon's castle.

The Special World

Shrek enters his special world as soon as he leaves his swamp with Donkey. This world is full of adventure in faraway lands.

Allies and Enemies

Donkey decides to join Shrek on his adventure. Even though Shrek pretends not to like Donkey, deep down he is really glad Donkey is his friend. Lord Farquaad is his main enemy. Some may say the Dragon is also an enemy but she is really an obstacle Shrek must overcome.

Tests and Challenges

While it might seem Shrek's biggest challenge is to rescue Fiona from the fire-breathing Dragon, it turns out that his real test is to learn to trust and love other people. Instead of always pushing people away, Shrek must learn to open his heart to Donkey and Fiona so that he can feel love and friendship.

Slaying the Dragon

Even though Shrek manages to rescue the Princess from the Dragon, his biggest fear is yet to be overcome. Shrek is secretly in love with Fiona. It's not until he works up the courage to tell her how he feels that he slays his dragon.

The Reward

His reward comes when the sun goes down and Fiona turns into an ogre just like Shrek. He discovers that no matter how people look on the outside, it is what is inside that counts.

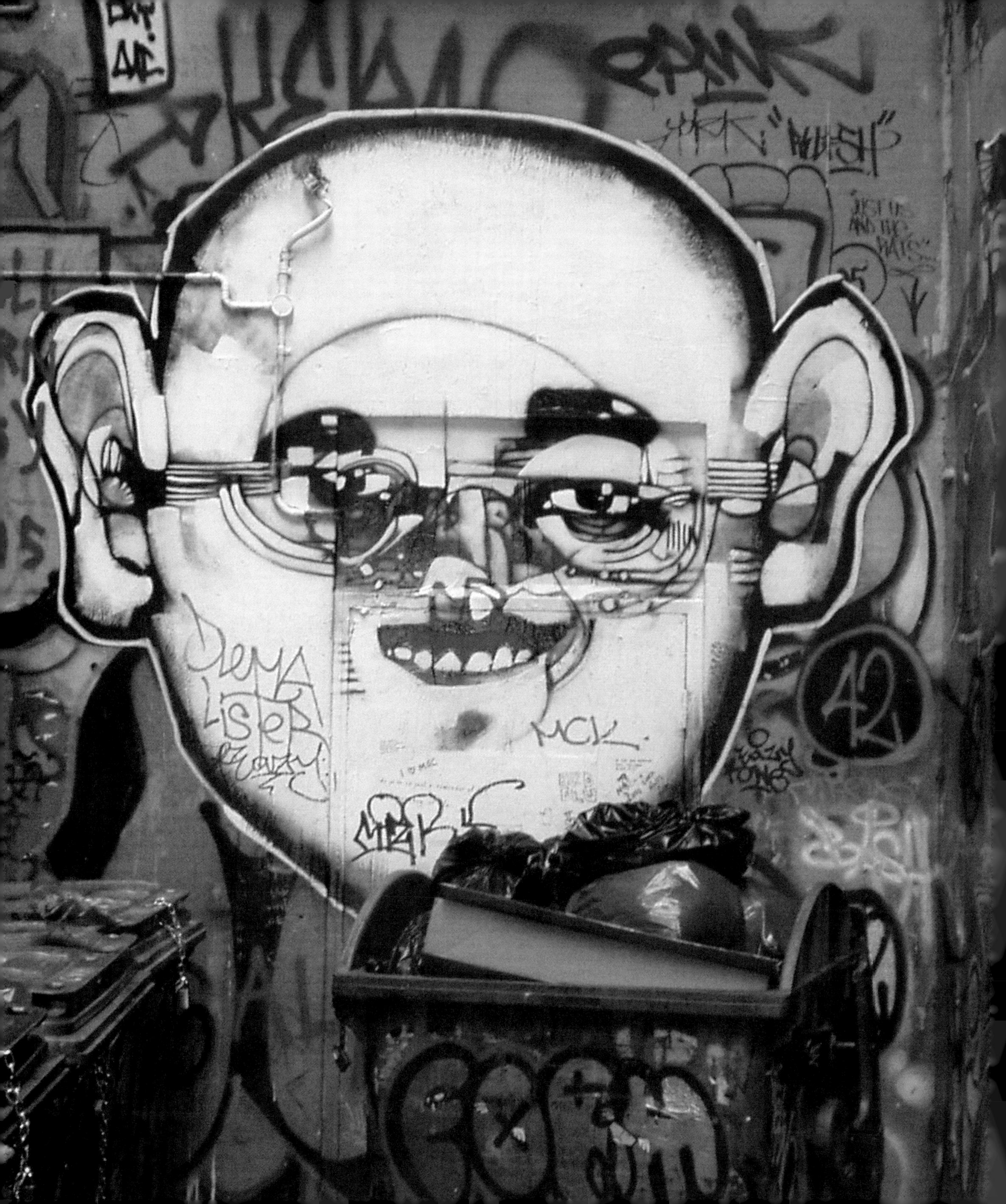
MCK
42

SUMMARY: SLAYING THE DRAGON

- *There is nothing wrong with fear*
- *Just do the best you can*
- *Learn to understand fear*
- *Failure is part of the journey*
- *Talking to yourself can help*
- *Sometimes life is tough*
- *Allies can help, but you must slay your own dragons*
- *Peel back the layers and live life to the full*

THE

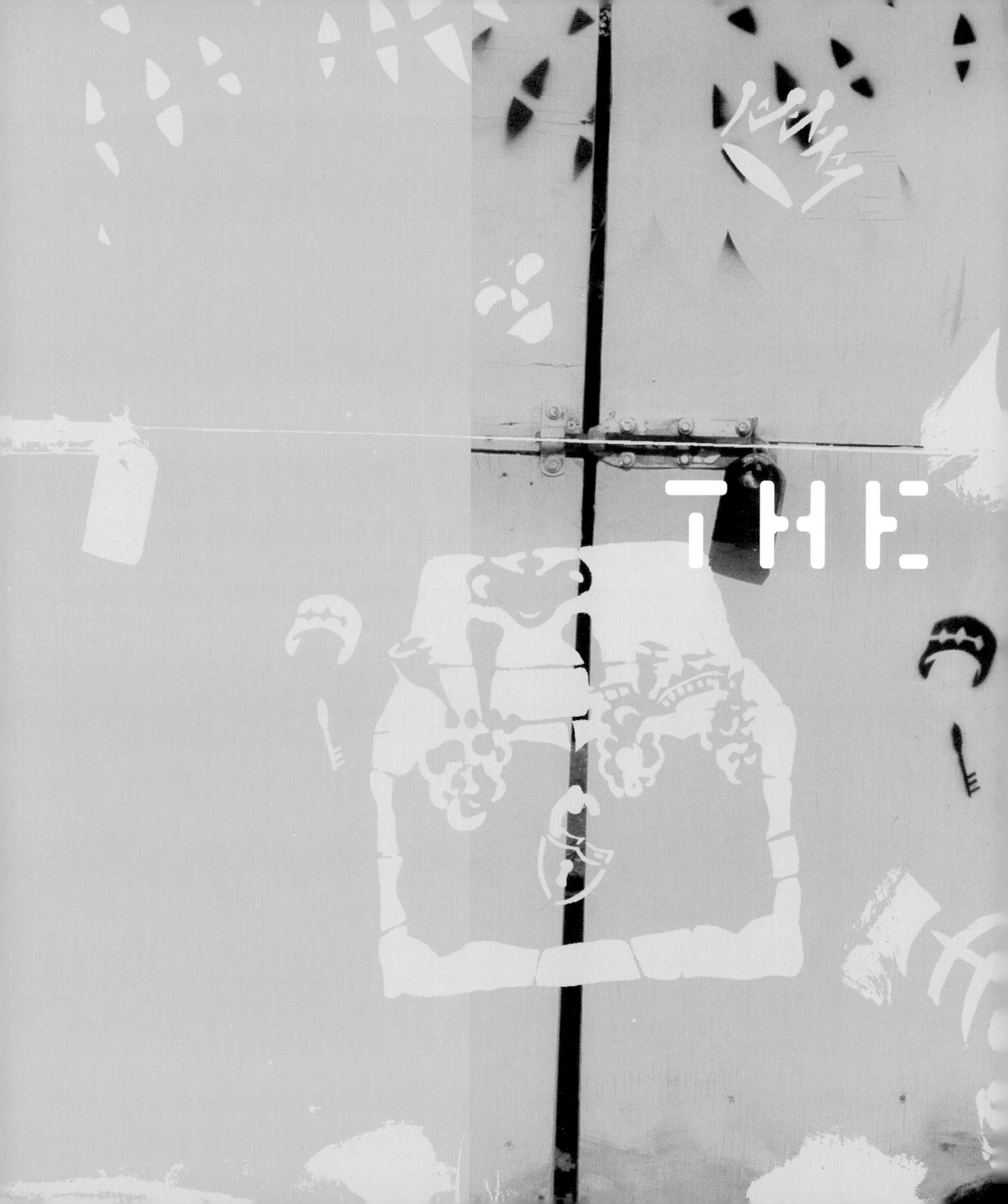

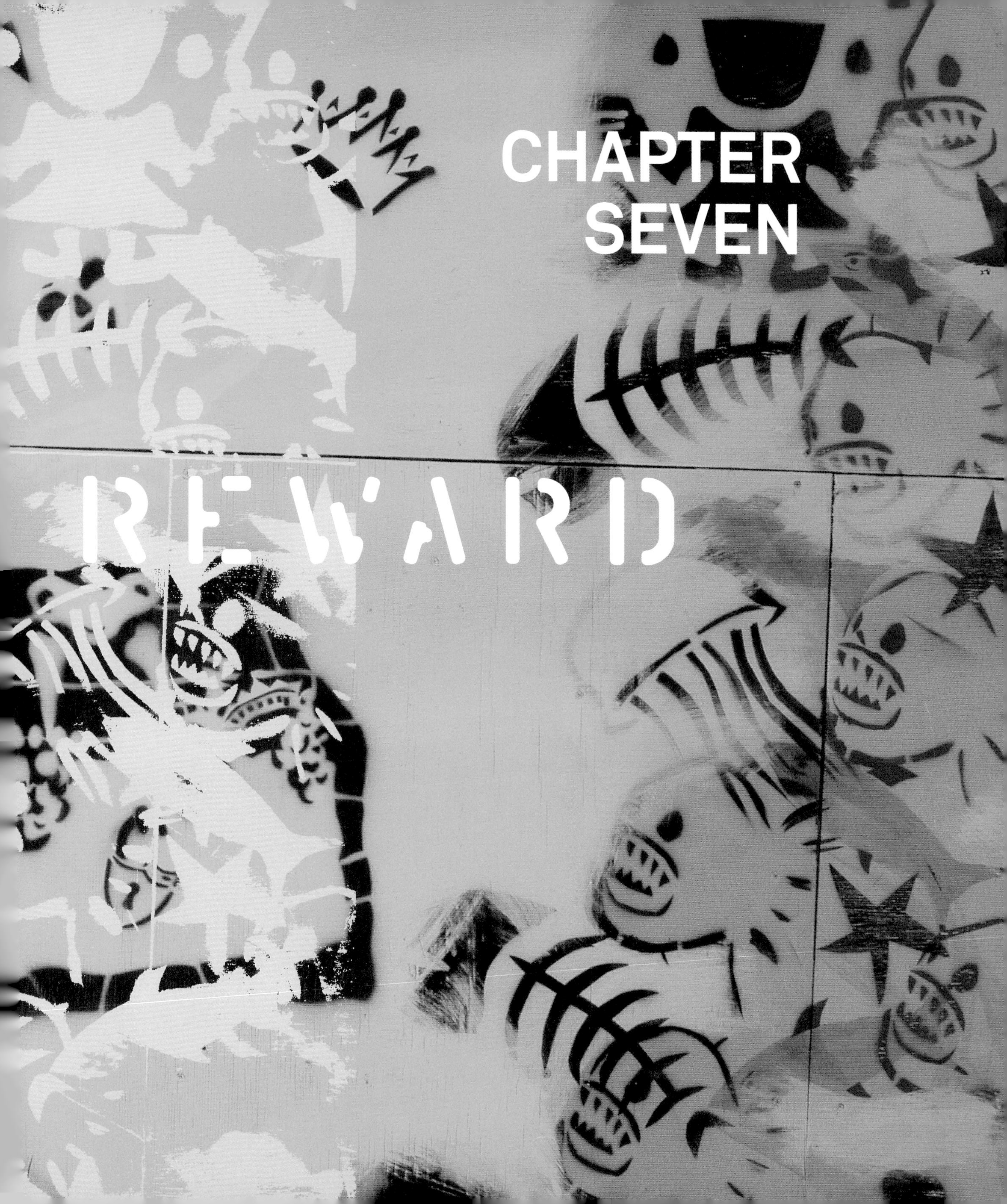

CHAPTER SEVEN

REWARD

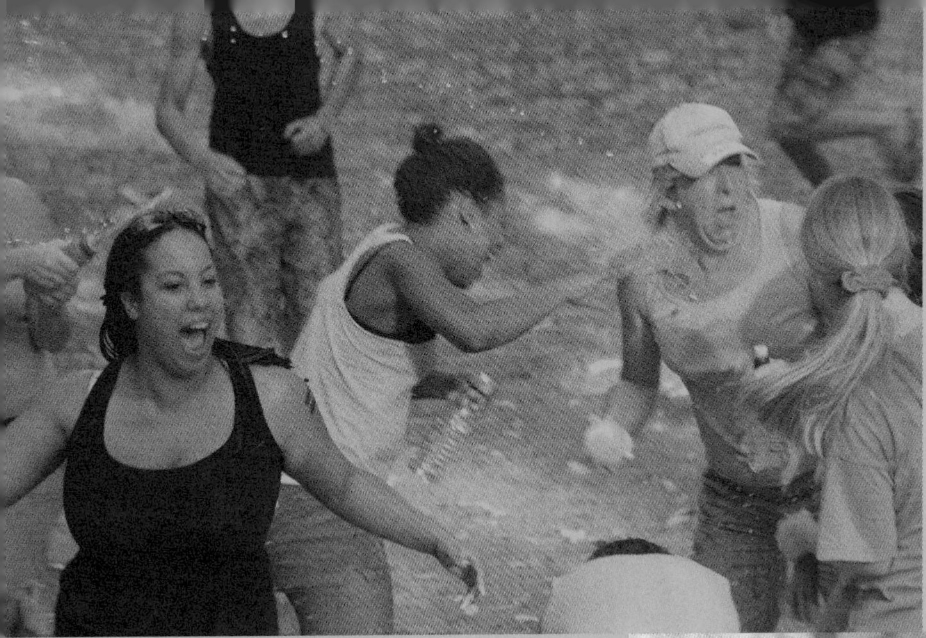

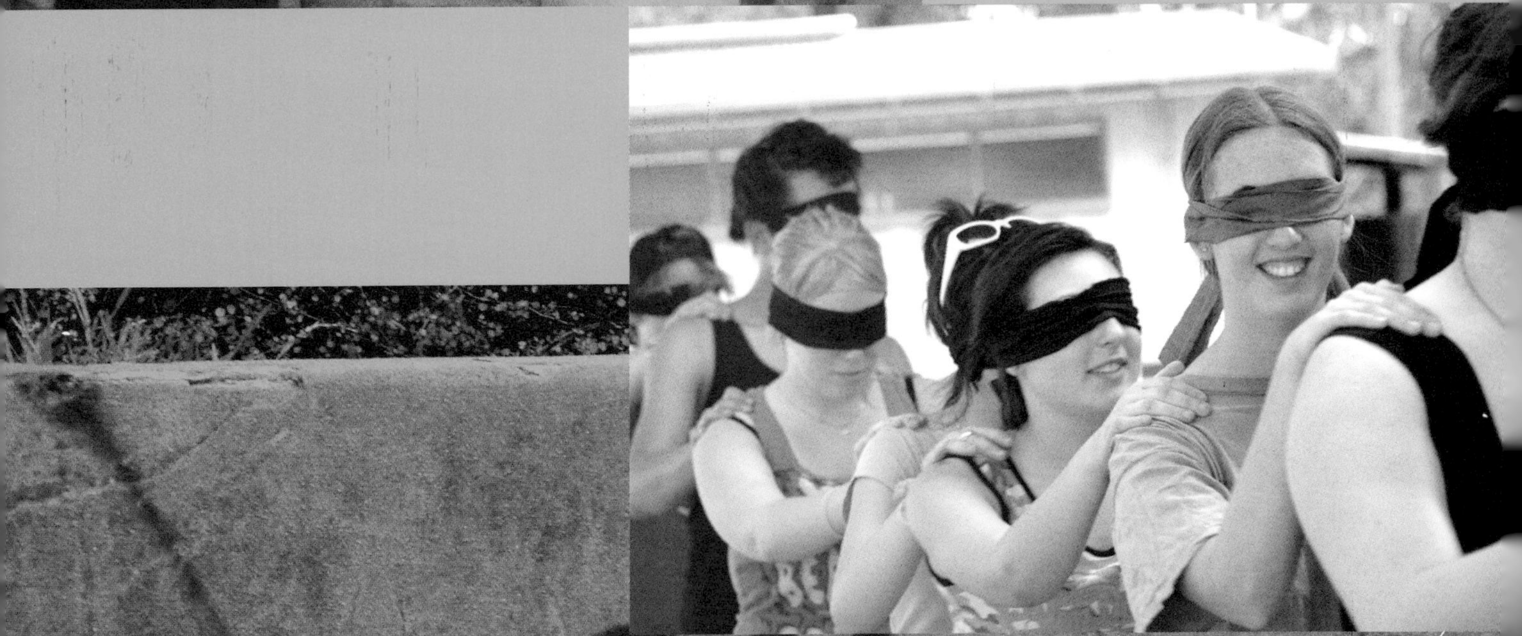

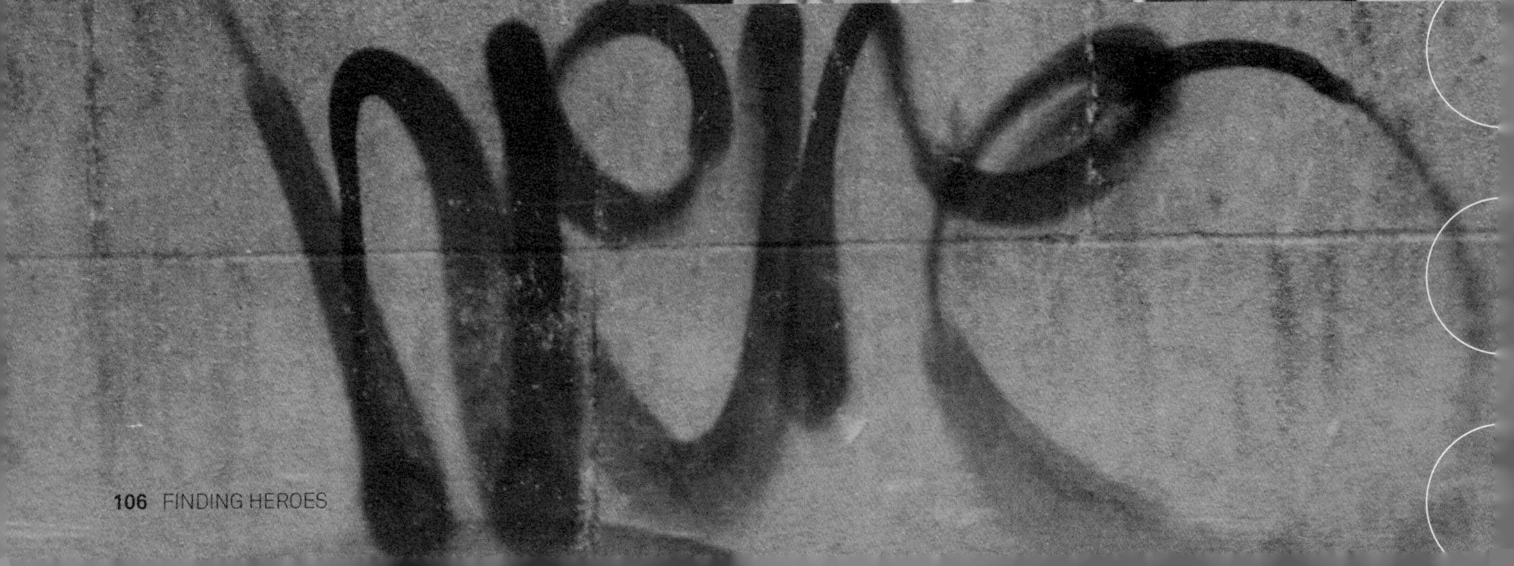

The reward and return

Having slain the dragon and overcome our fears, we have earned the right to gain our rewards in the journey of life. Funnily enough, the rewards are not always what we expect.

Rather than winning trophies and awards, what we often end up with is emotional positiveness, which comes in the following ways.

Enduring a long journey teaches us:

- **Self Belief** – the belief that **we can** do almost anything we set our minds to
- Self Awareness – the understanding of why we act the way we do
- Self Discipline – the personal strength to keep going when things are hard
- Self-esteem – the strength to believe in ourselves no matter what others think
- Self Control – the ability to decide how we feel.

Once we have all of these in place, life seems to become more enjoyable, and often we can redirect our energy to helping others.

THE GIFT OF THE JOURNEY IS INNER PEACE

Rewards Are Often Planned

To gain rewards, we often need to set goals to help us get there. There are many steps in life's journey, but the best way to make goals work for us is to start writing them down and mapping our progress.

Are your goals SMART goals?

- ☑ **Specific**
- ☑ **Measurable**
- ☑ **Achievable**
- ☑ **Realistic**
- ☑ **Time frame**

How to set goals:

- Set yourself a clear achievable task.
- Write it down on a piece of paper or in a diary.
- List the five small steps you will need to take in order to reach that goal.
- Set timeframes on each of those steps.
- START.

Goals are a great way of getting us out of our comfort zone and into action. Goals keep us honest. And by writing them down, we can't just forget about them!

Living without goals is like going shopping without a list.

HERO: LLEYTON HEWITT

Champion tennis player Lleyton Hewitt and his then coach, Roger Rashid, set themselves the goal of winning the Australian Open in 2005. As Hewitt said:

'I would have given anything to be in this position, to have an opportunity to play one match for the title here in Melbourne. Now part of that dream's come true. I know as well as anyone that I'm going to have to go out there and play one of my best matches to get up against Marat. But at least I've put myself in a position to have a crack at it.'

In the end Hewitt lost the match, but that did not make him a loser. Setting goals and trying your best to achieve them is reward enough in itself.

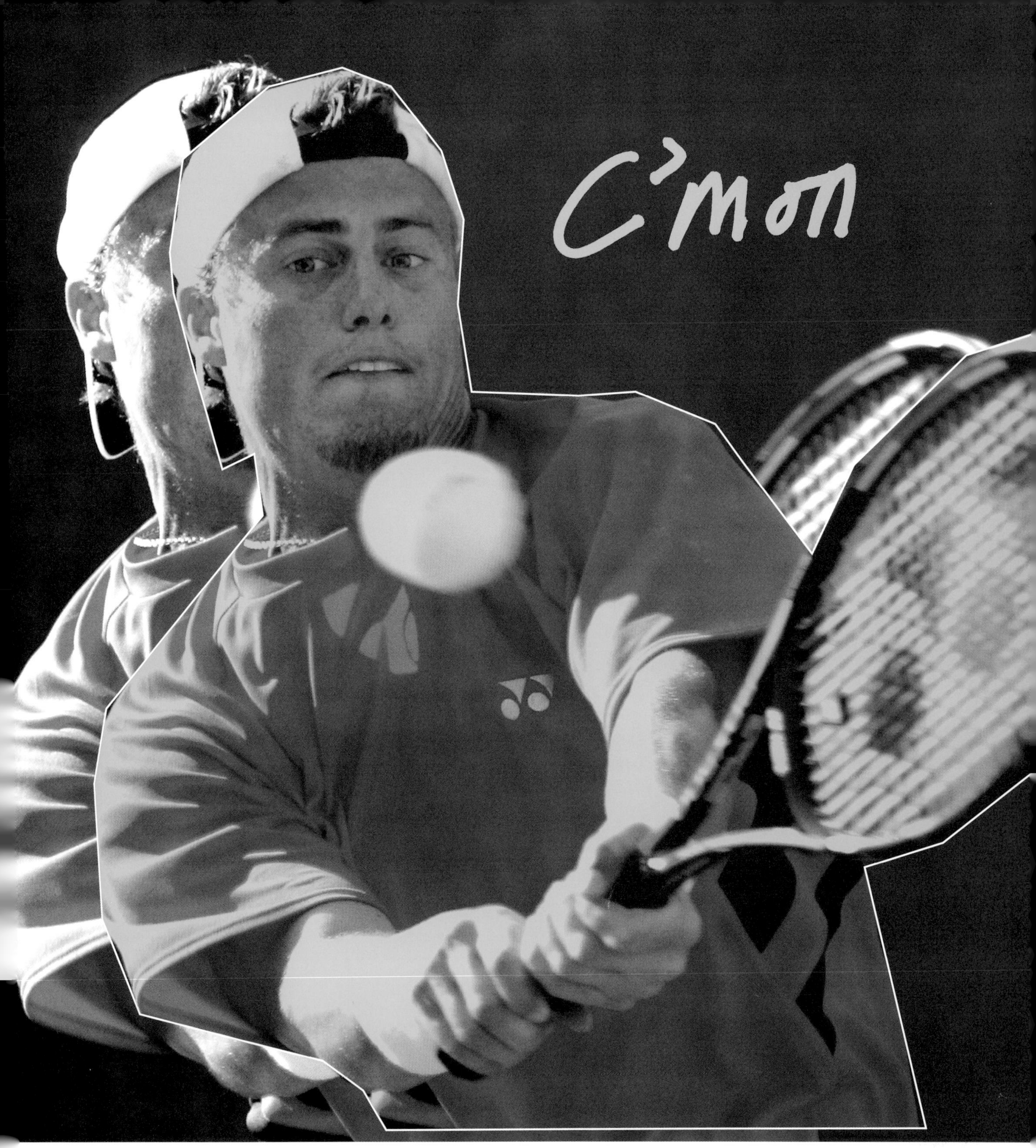
C'mon

Balance Is a Great Reward

We are all different, and we all have different ways of expressing things. Some of us will paint, some of us will dance, some will cook, others will sing. Some will play sport while others prefer to read books. Whatever the case, there is always a way for us to express ourselves.

Find Your Favourite Activities and Perfect Them

Finding our favourite activities is great fun. Often it takes many years, but the fun is in the journey. To help find this balance in life, try a few of the following things and see which ones you enjoy most.

If you enjoy telling jokes, singing, writing plays and poetry, listening to people speaking, you have a strong **Verbal Intelligence**.

If so, start playing around with these ideas:

- working in radio
- becoming an actor
- becoming a speech writer
- sports broadcasting
- telling jokes
- writing for a newspaper.

If you really enjoy working with large-scale ideas, perhaps you have a strong **Spatial Intelligence**.

If so, start playing around with these ideas:

- designing your own city
- creating a life-sized sculpture
- painting a life-sized portrait
- designing your own maze
- designing a skyscraper.

If you really enjoy working with numbers, perhaps you have a strong **Mathematical Intelligence**.

If so, start playing around with these ideas:

- working with computers
- doing Mum and Dad's tax return
- opening your own bank account
- becoming a spy who cracks codes.

If you really enjoy working with sounds and rhythms, perhaps you have a strong **Musical Intelligence**.

If so, start playing around with these ideas:

- playing an instrument
- learning to dance

- composing an opera
- starting a band
- conducting an orchestra
- building a CD collection.

If you really enjoy being physically active, then perhaps you have a strong **Physical Intelligence**.

If so, start playing around with these ideas:
- joining a sports team
- going dancing
- rebuilding an old engine
- running a marathon
- going for a hike
- becoming a professional athlete.

If you really enjoy being alone and thinking things through for yourself, then perhaps you have a strong **Personal Intelligence**.

If so, start playing around with these ideas:
- writing a diary
- meditating
- writing a book
- studying philosophy
- becoming a personal development teacher.

Whichever of these we tend towards, it is important that we understand we are all made up of multiple intelligences. So while we might be good at singing, it also helps to develop our song writing. While we might be good at athletics, it also helps to develop our personal concentration.

Finding balance is not just about doing the things we do well. It is about trying things which challenge us too.

The reward is in the challenge, not the result.

HERO: BILL GATES

Bill Gates, the American billionaire and founder of Microsoft, has spent his life building a computer empire. But he has also spent close to a billion dollars on providing vaccinations for the poor in Africa. While he spent his life building a computer empire, many of his rewards have come in other ways.

Even a man as rich as Bill Gates finds it hard to gain happiness from a life which does not involve helping others.

Give Something Back

There is a very old saying from the Bible which says:

As ye sow, so shall ye reap.

Just as it is impossible to gain the reward of eating fresh fruit without first planting and tending to a fruit tree, so too it is important that we balance our lives by planting the seeds of success early.

As we have learned, there are many steps on the journey of life. We are like everything else on the planet. Our lives go in cycles and good things take time. To really gain rewards in life, often we have to work hard for a long time. Like a tree which grows up strong, we have to allow our 'roots' to go deep into the earth before we can grow upwards.

Also, like a tree, eventually we have to start giving back.

Trees grow fruit. Fruit grows seeds. Seeds grow more trees.

Five Ways You Can Give Back

· Help someone on their first day at school.
· Clean up your bedroom.
· Tell your parents you love them.
· Write a letter to your grandparents.
· Take a young brother or sister to the movies.

The reward is in the challenge, not the result.

FILM: FINDING NEMO

The Ordinary World

Nemo is a clownfish, born on the Great Barrier Reef, who lives with his father. Nemo's mother, brothers and sisters were taken by a barracuda, so Nemo's father, Marlin, is overprotective of him. Nemo is raised in a loving but very sheltered environment.

The Call to Adventure

Nemo's call to adventure comes one day while on a school excursion, when he decides he wants to do some exploring of his own. Given a dare by his new school friends, Nemo swims out into the open sea, where he is captured by a diver.

Enemies and Allies

Hearing the news, Nemo's father Marlin swings into action and tries to follow the speedboat. Along the way he is sidetracked by Bruce, a great white shark. Meanwhile Nemo finds himself in an aquarium where he meets a group of new friends who start plotting his escape.

Tests and Challenges

Marlin finds out where Nemo is, and heads south towards Sydney. Along the way he is challenged by jellyfish and helped by pelicans! Eventually even Nemo gets to hear that his father is coming to save him.

Slaying the Dragon

Nemo's chance to escape comes earlier than he expected, and he manages to make it into the harbour where he is reunited with his father. His final hurdle comes when his father's friend Dory becomes trapped in a fisherman's net. With all his cunning, Nemo manages to free Dory.

The Reward

In the end, Nemo and his father learn to trust each other and let go of the past to open up a brave new future together.

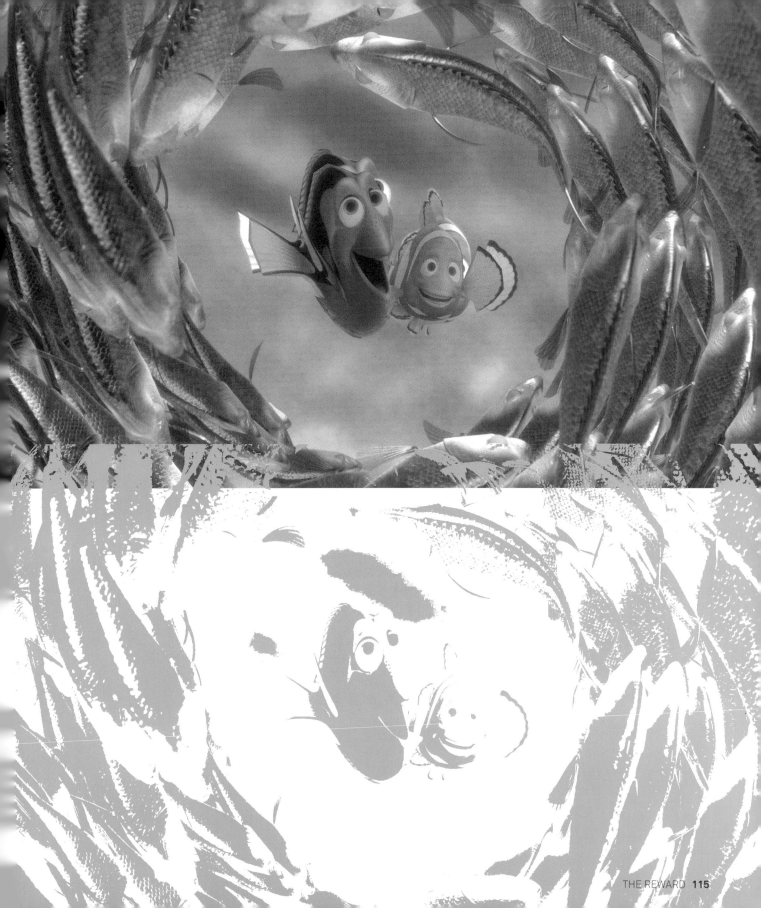

As we will learn as we get older, as soon as one journey ends, another begins. Very often we are on several journeys at once.

The Lord of the Rings is a great example of a journey which never ends. Throughout the story, the heroes find themselves tested time and time again, yet after each test there always seems to be a new challenge.

This is the same with life. Challenges never stop, and neither does our learning.

Read the following if you need to be convinced:

- 80% of children in Year 5 this year will enter a career which does not even exist right now.
- The amount of information in the world doubles every two years.
- 90% of the information and knowledge you will require by the time you leave school has not been invented yet.

So as we embark on our journey, let's always remember that it is okay to make mistakes. It is okay to be different and to strive to make a difference in the world. It is okay to have fun, and above all it is okay to love. Everyone is already a hero. You are intelligent in so many ways, so just get out there and get into it. Forget about trying to be perfect ... and just try and be you.

Good luck.

As one journey ends another begins

SUMMARY: THE REWARD

- *Rewards are often planned*
- *Set goals, write them down, and start!*
- *Balance is a great reward*
- *The gift of the journey is inner peace*
- *Accept yourself for who you are*
- *Find your favourite activities and perfect them*
- *The reward is in the challenge, not the result*
- *Give something back*
- *As one journey ends, another begins*

PICTURE CREDITS

Page 1: Liz Ellis, courtesy of Netball Australia

Page 5: from *Antz*, courtesy of Austral

Page 7: from *Lion King*, courtesy of Austral

Page 11: from left, Jane Ilitch, Liz Ellis, Irene van Dyk (NZ), Alison Broadbent, photograph by Heath Gibson, courtesy of Netball Australia

Page 14: Sarah Ryan dives from blocks at Olympic Aquatic Centre during training session for 2004 Games in Athens, August 11, photographer by Colleen Petch, Newspix.com

Page 17: from *Diary of Anne Frank*, courtesy of Austral

Page 21: from *Charlie and the Chocolate Factory*, courtesy of Austral

Page 33: Martin Luther King waves to supporters in this 28 August 1963 file photo, from the Lincoln Memorial on the Mall in Washington DC, during the 'March on Washington', Newspix.com

Page 41–2: from *Chicken Run*, courtesy of Austral

Page 49: Louise Sauvage first in the women's 800 m wheelchair final, 29 August 2003, during the 9th IAAF World Athletics Championships at the Stade de France in Saint-Denis outside of Paris, photograph by Jeff Haynes, Newspix.com

Page 55: from *Wizard of Oz*, courtesy of Austral

Page 66: Guy Sebastian in concert in Brisbane, 2005, photograph by Dane Beesley, Newspix.com

Page 69: Craig Stevens (left) and Ian Thorpe, photograph by Gregg Porteous, Newspix.com

Page 75, 83: Britney Spears sings at Fox Studios in the lead up to her movie premiere *Cross Roads*, 18/4/02, photograph by Renee Nowytarger, Newspix.com

Page 77: Nelson Mandela, courtesy of Jon Carnegie

Page 81: Brigitte Muir during a climbing expedition on 04/05/90, photograph by John Feder, Newspix.com

Page 85: from *Harry Potter and the Philosopher's Stone*, courtesy of Austral

Page 94: Ernest Shackleton's ship, *Endurance*, crushed by ice during Antarctic expedition February 1915, Newspix.com

Page 100: from *Shrek*, courtesy of Austral

Page 109: Lleyton Hewitt at the 2005 US Open Tennis Championships, photograph by Timothy A. Clary, Newspix.com

Page 115: from *Finding Nemo*, courtesy of Austral

Photographs of graffiti throughout are by Nick Mau.

All other photographs are courtesy of the Reach Foundation.

QUOTES

LIZ ELLIS http://www.womenlawyers.org.au/ellis.htm

GRANT HACKETT http://www.girlfriend.com.au/navitron/display.cfm?objectid=1496D7DA-77CB427BBF8D21FFDF513042&navid=D38B513D-3D65-4D6C-A6D5B5237F5E48F8

MARTIN LUTHER KING from <u>The Secrets of the Great Communicators</u>, Peter Thompson, ABC Books p34

LLEYTON HEWITT
http://www.lleytonhewitt.biz/shanghai02int.htm
http://www.theage.com.au/news/Tennis/The-one-Lleyton-wants/2005/01/30/1106850165996.html

BRITNEY SPEARS
http://search.barnesandnoble.com/booksearch/isbninquiry.asp?userid=Hg3MciHBNj&ean=9780609807019&displayonly=EXC#EXC

NELSON MANDELA 1994 Inaugural Address, Original source : Marianne Williamson 1992.
A Return to Love: Reflections on the Principles of a course in Miracles, Aquarian.

BILL GATES
http://www.earlytorise.com/_pages/_messages/wise_543.html

ABOUT THE AUTHORS

JIM STYNES was born in Ireland in 1966 and arrived in Australia in 1984 to try out for the Melbourne Football Club. Jim went on to win the Brownlow Medal, the AFL's highest player honour, and to establish the record for the number of consecutive games played. In 1994 Jim co-founded the Reach Foundation, which is fast becoming one of the most influential educational institutions in the country. As a result of his work with youth, Jim has been awarded the White Flame Award and was also a member of the Youth Suicide Task Force and the Federal Minister for Youth's Advisory forum. He won Entrepreneur of the Year 2004, and was Victorian of the Year in 2001 and 2003. Jim lives in Melbourne with his wife Sam, daughter Matisse and son Tiernan. www.jimstynes.com

DR JON CARNEGIE trained and worked as a teacher in Melbourne before heading overseas for several years to pursue a career as a writer. He started teaching at Melbourne's Trinity Grammar in 1995 and runs highly successful self-development workshops in schools at both primary and secondary levels. Jon's innovative teaching technique won him the John O. Miller Award for Excellence in Education (2000), and the Commonwealth Teachers Prize for Excellence and the National Excellence Award for Secondary Teaching in 2001. He runs his own school in Melbourne, the Carnegie Education Centre, where his doctoral study on middle school transitional programs forms the basis of the Carnegie Education curriculum. Jon was responsible for bringing Nelson Mandela to Australia in 2000 and was the only Australian delegate at the International Boys' School Coalition (2005), speaking with the likes of Madeleine Albright. He lives in Melbourne with his wife Catherine and they are expecting their first child in 2006. www.ce.edu.au

Jim Stynes and Jon Carnegie are the authors, with Paul Currie, of the best-selling *Heroes* (Allen & Unwin, 2003). Jon co-authored Trisha Broadbridge's remarkable story, *Beyond the Wave* (2005).

ACKNOWLEDGEMENTS

To Paul Currie who co-authored *Heroes* and who first developed the hero's journey concept with us — you are one of the most creative geniuses of our time.

To all the teachers who have encouraged us to write this book, shared our dream and showed so much enthusiasm for developing the person as well as the curriculum — thanks, and keep up the good work.

To everyone who has been part of the Reach dream since its formation in 1994 — you are the inspiration for this book.

Finally, to our wives and families, Catherine Carnegie and one soon-to-be-born son, and Sam Stynes and kids Matisse and Tiernan — thank you for all your love, understanding and wisdom. You are our heroes.

FINDING THE HEROES IN THIS BOOK